Terry Joh

Piano/Forte

Methuen Drama

Published by Methuen Drama 2006

3 5 7 9 10 8 6 4 2

Methuen Drama
A & C Black Publishers Limited
38 Soho Square
London W1D 3HB
www.acblack.com

ISBN: 978-0-7136-8283-0

A CIP catalogue record for this book is available from the British Library

Typeset by Country Setting, Kingsdown, Kent
Printed and bound in Great Britain by MPG Books Ltd, Bodmin, Cornwall

Caution

ROYAL COURT

Royal Court Theatre presents

PIANO/FORTE

by **Terry Johnson**

First performance at the Royal Court Jerwood Theatre Downstairs,
Sloane Square, London on 14 September 2006.

Supported by
**Nica Burns and Max Weitzenhoffer
for Nimax Theatres**

PIANO/FORTE

by **Terry Johnson**

Caterina **Nuria Benet**
Clifford **Oliver Cotton**
Juan **Sebastian Gonzalez**
Louise **Kelly Reilly**
Dawn **Natalie Walter**
Ray **Danny Webb**
Abigail **Alicia Witt**

Director **Terry Johnson**
Designer **Mark Thompson**
Lighting Designer **Simon Corder**
Sound Designer **Ian Dickinson**
Assistant Director **Vicky Jones**
Casting **Lisa Makin**
Production Manager **Paul Handley**
Stage Manager **Ba Penney**
Deputy Stage Manager **Nicole Keighley**
Assistant Stage Manager **Patrick Birch**
Stage Management Work Placements
Lottie Cousins, Kate Hall
Dialect Coach **Alison Mackinnon**
Aerial Choreographer **Gaynor Derbyshire**
Costume Supervisor **Laura Hunt**
Flying **Flying by Foy Ltd**
Set Built by **Miraculous Engineering**
Set Painted by **Magnus Irvin**

The Royal Court and Stage Management wish to thank the following for their help with this
production: Cadogan Hall.

Make up provided by MAC

THE COMPANY

Terry Johnson (writer & director)
For the Royal Court: Hitchcock Blonde, Hysteria, Cries from the Mammal House, Insignificance.
As director: Dumb Show.
Other plays include: Cleo Camping Emmanuelle and Dick (National); Dead Funny (Hampstead/ Vaudeville/West End/tour); Imagine Drowning (Hampstead); Tuesday's Child (Theatre Royal, Stratford); Unsuitable for Adults, Amabel (Bush); Days Here So Dark (Paines Plough).
As director: The Graduate (Gielgud/Plymouth Theater, Broadway); One Flew Over the Cuckoo's Nest, Entertaining Mr Sloane (West End); The London Cuckolds, Sparkleshark (National); The Memory of Water (Hampstead/ Vaudeville); Elton John's Glasses (Palace Theatre, Watford/Queen's); Cracked (Hampstead); The Libertine (Steppenwolf, Chicago); Just Between Ourselves, Ragdoll (Bristol Old Vic); Death of a Salesman (Theatre Royal, York).
Adaptations include: The London Cuckolds (National).
Television includes: Cor Blimey!, Way Upstream, Neville's Island, Not Only But Always.
Terry is literary associate at the Royal Court.

Nuria Benet
Theatre includes: XXX Anonymous (Prague Festival); I Confess (Hoxton Hall); Maker-Do (The Place); Nuts Coconuts (Edinburgh International Festival); El Libertino (Teatro de la Abadía, Madrid); The Firebird (Octagon, Bolton); Let's Charleston (tour); Goblin Feast, The Snowflake Princess (Komedia, Brighton/tour); Cinderella (tour); Aladdin (Eye Theatre, Suffolk); La Devoción de la Cruz (Sala Valle-Inclán, Madrid); Salvage/Love (Union); El Quijote! (Gate); Death of the Lorquian Woman (Lion and Unicorn); Pledges, Vows, Pass This Note (Etcetera); Beauty and the Beast (BAC); The Suspicious Truth (Bloomsbury); In Five Year's Time (Southwark Playhouse).
Television includes: Mighty Truck of Stuff, The Bill, Hospital Central.
Film includes: El Inglés, The Visit, Baby Snatcher, Thinking Aloud.
Radio includes: The Psychology of Dangerous Roads, Andalus.

Simon Corder (lighting designer)
For the Royal Court: Hitchcock Blonde, I Licked A Slag's Deodorant.
Other theatre includes: Creatures of the Night (Night Safari, Singapore); Aladdin (Capitol, Horsham); To Kill a Mockingbird (Theatr Clwyd);

Entertaining Mr Sloane (Theatre Royal, Bath/ West End); Les Enfants du Paradis (RSC); Cleo Camping Emmanuelle and Dick, The London Cuckolds, The Ends of the Earth (National); A Streetcar Named Desire (West End); The Misanthrope, American Buffalo (Young Vic); The Robbers (Gate); The Letter (Lyric); After Darwin (Hampstead); A Hard Heart, Hippolytos (Almeida).
Opera includes: Die Zauberflöte, Manon Lescaut (Teatro Regio, Parma); Pique Dame (Teatro alla Scala, Milan); Die Entführung aus dem Serail (Teatro della Muse, Ancona); Poppea (Opera Theatre Company of Ireland); Cunning Little Vixen, Falstaff (ETO); Rodelinda (Opera Touring Company/Brooklyn Academy of Arts, USA); Il Trovatore (Ravenna Festival); Don Giovanni (Holland Park Opera); Carmen, A Village Romeo and Juliet (Teatro Lirico, Cagliari); Mephistopheles (ENO/Colon, Buenos Aires); Aida (London/Seville/Lisbon/Helsinki/Buenos Aires); The Vanishing Bridegroom (Scottish Opera); The Blackened Man (Buxton Festival/ Linbury).
Dance includes: 3 (The Cholmondeleys); The Featherstonehaughs Draw on the Sketchbooks of Egon Schiele (The Featherstonehaughs); Kohle Körper (Tanzlandschaft Ruhr); Vom Zorne Des Achilleus, Yerma, Carmen (Tanz-Forum, Oper der Stadt Köln).
Film & Television includes: Riot at the Rite, Double Take, Speed Ramp, The Lost Dances of Egon Schiele.
Other work includes: Cascade (The Alnwick Garden, Northumberland); Bough 2 (Radiance Festival, Glasgow); Bough I (Oxo Wharf, London); Standing Still (Sherwood Forest).

Oliver Cotton
For the Royal Court: Lear, Bingo, Man is Man, The Duchess of Malfi, The Tutor, Erogenous Zones, Captain Oates' Left Sock, The Local Stigmatic, The Enoch Show.
Other theatre includes: The Royal Hunt of the Sun, Summerfolk, The Villain's Opera, Money, Troilus & Cressida, Piano, The Crucible, Despatches, The World Turned Upside Down, Half Life, The Passion, The Force of Habit, The Madras House (National); Philadelphia Story, Richard II (Old Vic); The Crucible (Birmingham Rep/tour); Brand (RSC/Haymarket); Some Americans Abroad, The Plain Dealer, Richard III, Edward IV, Henry VI, The Marrying of Ann Leete (RSC); Twelfth Night (Globe); Blast from the Past

(West Yorkshire Playhouse); Educating Rita (Sheffield Playhouse); Skylight (Auckland Theatre); King Lear (Southwark Playhouse); Butterfly Kiss (Almeida); That Summer (Hampstead); The Speakers (ICA); Cato Street (Young Vic); An Ideal Husband (Lyric); Benefactors (Vaudeville); Children of a Lesser God (Albery); The Homecoming (Garrick).

Television includes: Doctors, Midsomer Murders, M.I.T., Judge John Deed, Innocents, Preston Front, Rhodes, Sharpe's Battle, The Year of the French, Robin of Sherwood, Room at the Bottom, David Copperfield, The Party, The Borgias, Redemption, Westbeach, Fireworks, The Camomile Lawn, Hotel Babylon, Sensitive Skin.

Film includes: The Dancer Upstairs, Baby Blue, Beowulf, The Opium War, The Innocent Sleep, Son of the Pink Panther, Christopher Columbus, Hiding Out, The Sicilian, Eleni, Firefox, Oliver Twist, The Day Christ Died, The Mulberry Bush, Here We Go Round, Colour Me Kubrick.

Ian Dickinson (sound designer)
For the Royal Court: Rock 'n' Roll, Motortown, Rainbow Kiss, The Winterling, Alice Trilogy, Fewer Emergencies, Way to Heaven, The Woman Before, Stoning Mary (& Drum Theatre, Plymouth), Breathing Corpses, Wild East, Dumb Show, Shining City (& Gate, Dublin), Lucky Dog, Blest Be the Tie (with Talawa), Ladybird, Notes on Falling Leaves, Loyal Women, The Sugar Syndrome, Blood, Playing the Victim (with Told By an Idiot), Fallout, Flesh Wound, Hitchcock Blonde (& Lyric), Black Milk, Crazyblackmuthafuckin'self, Caryl Churchill Shorts, Push Up, Fucking Games, Herons.

Other theatre includes: Pillars of the Community (National); A Few Good Men (Haymarket); Port, As You Like It, Poor Superman, Martin Yesterday, Fast Food, Coyote Ugly (Royal Exchange, Manchester); Night of the Soul (RSC/Barbican); Eyes of the Kappa (Gate); Crime & Punishment in Dalston (Arcola); Search & Destroy (New End); The Whore's Dream (RSC/Edinburgh).

Ian is Head of Sound at the Royal Court.

Sebastian Gonzalez
Theatre includes: Peter Pan (Chicken Shed/Duke of York's); Stomp (La Cigalle, Paris); Romeo and Juliet, Brave New World, Sleeping Beauty, A Christmas Carol, Knight before Christmas, A Midsummer Night's Dream (Chicken Shed); Hamlet (The Old Bull/The Rotunda).
Dance includes: Globaleyes (Chicken Shed/Royal

Lyceum, Edinburgh); Men in the Wall (3D dance video installation, ICA); Die Orchidee in Plastik Karton, Reverse Effect (South Bank Centre); Nada Pessoal (Teatro Nacional, Brazil); No Instante (Bonnie Bird/Teatro Nacional, Brazil/ The Place); Rite of Spring (Cochrane); Divagate (Gardner Arts Centre/South Bank Centre/ Lemon Tree/Duncan Centre, Prague/German tour); Il Puritani (Gardner Arts Centre).
Television includes: Happy Birthday Peter Pan, Behind the Shed, The King's Web.

Vicky Jones (assistant director)
As assistant director for the Royal Court: The One With The Oven, Rampage, I Remember the Royal Court.
As director theatre includes: The Freedom of the City (Finborough); Zoo (Arcola Festival); A Bedroom (Lyric Hammersmith Studio); The Blind Bird (Gate); Broken (Hen and Chickens); Airswimming, Laundry (Etcetera).
As assistant director theatre includes: See How They Run (tour/Duchess Theatre); Meeting Myself Coming Back (Soho); Habitats, The Flu Season (Gate); Big Voices (RSC); How Love Is Spelt (Summer Play Festival 2005, Off-Broadway); Journey's End (New Ambassador's Theatre).
Vicky is a director and tutor for the Royal Court Young Writers Programme.

Kelly Reilly
For the Royal Court: Blasted.
Other theatre includes: Look Back in Anger (Royal Lyceum, Edinburgh); After Miss Julie (Donmar); Sexual Perversity in Chicago (Comedy); A Prayer for Owen Meaney, The London Cuckolds (National); The Yalta Game (Gate, Dublin); The Graduate (Gielgud); Three Sisters (Oxford Stage Company tour/West End); Elton John's Glasses (Watford Palace).
Television includes: A for Andromeda, Poirot, The Safe House, Sex and Death, Wonderful You, Tom Jones, Poldark, Prime Suspect VI.
Film includes: Puffball, Mrs Henderson Presents, Pride and Prejudice, Les Poupees Russes, The Libertine, Dead Bodies, L'Auberge Espanol, Last Orders, Peaches, Maybe Baby.
Awards include: The London Critics' Circle Film Awards Best Newcomer 2006 for Mrs Henderson Presents; Empire Film Awards Best Newcomer 2006; Cannes Film Festival Best Newcomer 2005 for Les Poupees Russes.

Mark Thompson (designer)
For the Royal Court: Six Degrees of Separation (& Comedy), Hysteria (& Mark Taper Forum), The Kitchen, Neverland, Mouth to Mouth, Wild East, The Woman Before.
Other theatre includes: And Then There Were None (Gielgud); Mamma Mia! (Prince Edward's/Broadway); Art (Wyndham's/Broadway); Joseph and the Amazing Technicolor Dreamcoat (Palladium/Broadway); Shadowlands (Queen's/Broadway), The Lady in the Van (Queen's); Doctor Doolittle (Apollo); Blast, Bombay Dreams (Apollo/Broadway); Follies (Broadway); The Alchemist, Once in a Lifetime, Henry IV Parts 1 & 2, The Duchess of Malfi, Life x3, The Wind in the Willows, The Madness of George III, Arcadia, Pericles, What the Butler Saw, The Day I Stood Still (National); Measure for Measure, The Wizard of Oz, Much Ado About Nothing, A Comedy of Errors, Hamlet, The Unexpected Man (RSC); The Blue Room, Insignificance, Company, The Front Page (Donmar); Volpone, Betrayal, Party Time, Butterfly Kiss (Almeida).
Costumes include: Twelfth Night, Uncle Vanya (Donmar).
Opera includes: Falstaff (Scottish Opera); Peter Grimes (Opera North); Ariadne Auf Naxos (Salzburg); Il Viaggio a Reims (ROH); Hansel and Gretel (Sydney Opera House); The Two Windows (ENO); Queen of Spades (The Met, New York).
Film includes: The Madness of King George.
Awards include: 1990/1 Olivier Award, Plays and Players, and Critics' Award for The Wind in the Willows; 1992 Olivier Award for Set Design and Costume Design for Joseph and the Amazing Technicolor Dreamcoat and the Comedy of Errors; 1994 Olivier Award for Set Design for Hysteria; 1995 Critics' Circle Award for The Kitchen.

Natalie Walter
For the Royal Court: Ten Minutes of Human Rights.
Other theatre includes: Dead Funny (West Yorkshire Playhouse); The Ruffian on the Stair, Flanders Mare (Sound); As You Like It (Theatre Royal Bath/US tour); Constant Wife (Lyric, West End); Noises Off (National/West End); The Recruiting Officer (Chichester); Habeus Corpus (Donmar); The Brazen Age, The Bronze Age (Globe).
Television includes: Hollywood Goddesses, Hampstead Heath The Musical, Doctors, Babes in the Wood, The Peter Principle, Stalker's Apprentice, Road Rage, Get Well Soon, Perfect State, The Thin Blue Line, Harry Enfield and Chums.
Film includes: I Want Candy, Lady Godiva, Mary Loves Eddie, The Honey Trap, If Only, Remember Me.
Radio includes: Smelling of Roses, Chambers, No Commitments, All My Life, House of the Spirit Levels.

Danny Webb
For the Royal Court: Serious Money, Search and Destroy, Death and the Maiden, Dead Funny (& Vaudeville).
Other theatre includes: The Philanthropist (Donmar); The Green Man (Bush/Drum, Plymouth); Richard III (Crucible); One Flew Over the Cuckoo's Nest (tour); Art (Wyndham's); Hamlet (Leicester/tour); Popcorn (Apollo).
Television includes: Midsomer Murders, Rise and Fall of Rome, Dr Who II, Inspector Lynley, Nostradamus, Totally Frank, Hotel Babylon, Lewis, Heartbeat, A Touch of Frost, Silent Witness, My Family, Uncle Adolf, Murder in Suburbia, Dogma 3, Pepys, Life Begins, Murder Squad, Henry VIII, Cutting It, The Hound of the Baskervilles, Torch, Outside the Rules, Shackleton, McCready and Daughter, Take Me, The Knock, Hawk, Harbour Lights, Dalziel and Pascoe, Frenchman's Creek, Venus Hunters, The Jump, Out of Hours, 2.4 Children.
Film includes: The Harvester, The Aryan Couple, Stealing Lives, The Upside of Anger, Family Business, Shiner, In the Name of Love United, Still Crazy, Love and Death on Long Island, True Blue, Aliens III, Much the Miller Robin Hood, Henry V, Defence of the Realm, Billy the Kid and the Green Baize Vampire, The Year of the Quiet Sun, The Unapproachable, No Exit.

Alicia Witt
Theatre includes: The Shape of Things (New Ambassador's); The Gift (Tiffany Theater, Los Angeles).
Television includes: The Sopranos, Ally McBeal, Cybill, Passion's Way, Hotel Room, Twin Peaks.
Film includes: 88 Minutes, Last Holiday, The Upside of Anger, Two Weeks' Notice, Vanilla Sky, Ten Tiny Love Stories, Cecil B. Demented, Playing Mona Lisa, Urban Legend, Bongwater, Citizen Ruth, Four Rooms, Mr Holland's Opus, Fun, Bodies Rest and Motion, Liebestraum, Dune.
Awards include: U.S. Comedy Arts Festival Best Actress 2000 for Playing Mona Lisa; Sundance Film Festival Special Jury Recognition Award for Fun.

THE ENGLISH STAGE COMPANY AT THE ROYAL COURT

The English Stage Company at the Royal Court opened in 1956 as a subsidised theatre producing new British plays, international plays and some classical revivals.

The first artistic director George Devine aimed to create a writers' theatre, 'a place where the dramatist is acknowledged as the fundamental creative force in the theatre and where the play is more important than the actors, the director, the designer'. The urgent need was to find a contemporary style in which the play, the acting, direction and design are all combined. He believed that 'the battle will be a long one to continue to create the right conditions for writers to work in'.

photo: Stephen Cummiiskey

Devine aimed to discover 'hard-hitting, uncompromising writers whose plays are stimulating, provocative and exciting'. The Royal Court production of John Osborne's Look Back in Anger in May 1956 is now seen as the decisive starting point of modern British drama and the policy created a new generation of British playwrights. The first wave included John Osborne, Arnold Wesker, John Arden, Ann Jellicoe, N F Simpson and Edward Bond. Early seasons included new international plays by Bertolt Brecht, Eugène Ionesco, Samuel Beckett and Jean-Paul Sartre.

The theatre started with the 400-seat proscenium arch Theatre Downstairs, and in 1969 opened a second theatre, the 60-seat studio Theatre Upstairs. Some productions transfer to the West End, such as Tom Stoppard's Rock 'n' Roll, My Name is Rachel Corrie, Terry Johnson's Hitchcock Blonde, Caryl Churchill's Far Away and Conor McPherson's The Weir. Recent touring productions include Sarah Kane's 4.48 Psychosis (US tour) and Ché Walker's Flesh Wound (Galway Arts Festival). The Royal Court also co-produces plays which transfer to the West End or tour internationally, such as Conor McPherson's Shining City (with Gate Theatre, Dublin), Sebastian Barry's The Steward of Christendom and Mark Ravenhill's Shopping and Fucking (with Out of Joint), Martin McDonagh's The Beauty Queen Of Leenane (with Druid), Ayub Khan Din's East is East (with Tamasha).

Since 1994 the Royal Court's artistic policy has again been vigorously directed to finding and producing a new generation of playwrights. The writers include Joe Penhall, Rebecca Prichard, Michael Wynne, Nick Grosso, Judy Upton,

Meredith Oakes, Sarah Kane, Anthony Neilson, Judith Johnson, James Stock, Jez Butterworth, Marina Carr, Phyllis Nagy, Simon Block, Martin McDonagh, Mark Ravenhill, Ayub Khan Din, Tamantha Hammerschlag, Jess Walters, Ché Walker, Conor McPherson, Simon Stephens, Richard Bean, Roy Williams, Gary Mitchell, Mick Mahoney, Rebecca Gilman, Christopher Shinn, Kia Corthron, David Gieselmann, Marius von Mayenburg, David Eldridge, Leo Butler, Zinnie Harris, Grae Cleugh, Roland Schimmelpfennig, Chloe Moss, DeObia Oparei, Enda Walsh, Vassily Sigarev, the Presnyakov Brothers, Marcos Barbosa, Lucy Prebble, John Donnelly, Clare Pollard, Robin French, Elyzabeth Gregory Wilder, Rob Evans, Laura Wade, Debbie Tucker Green and Simon Farquhar. This expanded programme of new plays has been made possible through the support of A.S.K. Theater Projects and the Skirball Foundation, The Jerwood Charity, the American Friends of the Royal Court Theatre and (in 1994/5 and 1999) the National Theatre Studio.

The refurbished theatre in Sloane Square opened in February 2000, with a policy still inspired by the first artistic director George Devine. The Royal Court is an international theatre for new plays and new playwrights, and the work shapes contemporary drama in Britain and overseas.

The Royal Court's long and successful history of innovation has been built by generations of gifted and imaginative individuals. In 2006, the company celebrates its 50th Anniversary; an important landmark for the performing arts in Britain. For information on the many exciting ways you can help support the theatre, please contact the Development Department on 020 7565 5079.

AWARDS FOR
THE ROYAL COURT

Martin McDonagh won the 1996 George Devine Award, the 1996 Writers' Guild Best Fringe Play Award, the 1996 Critics' Circle Award and the 1996 Evening Standard Award for Most Promising Playwright for The Beauty Queen of Leenane. Marina Carr won the 19th Susan Smith Blackburn Prize (1996/7) for Portia Coughlan. Conor McPherson won the 1997 George Devine Award, the 1997 Critics' Circle Award and the 1997 Evening Standard Award for Most Promising Playwright for The Weir. Ayub Khan Din won the 1997 Writers' Guild Awards for Best West End Play and New Writer of the Year and the 1996 John Whiting Award for East is East (co-production with Tamasha).

Martin McDonagh's The Beauty Queen of Leenane (co-production with Druid Theatre Company) won four 1998 Tony Awards including Garry Hynes for Best Director. Eugene Ionesco's The Chairs (co-production with Theatre de Complicite) was nominated for six Tony awards. David Hare won the 1998 Time Out Live Award for Outstanding Achievement and six awards in New York including the Drama League, Drama Desk and New York Critics Circle Award for Via Dolorosa. Sarah Kane won the 1998 Arts Foundation Fellowship in Playwriting. Rebecca Prichard won the 1998 Critics' Circle Award for Most Promising Playwright for Yard Gal (co-production with Clean Break).

Conor McPherson won the 1999 Olivier Award for Best New Play for The Weir. The Royal Court won the 1999 ITI Award for Excellence in International Theatre. Sarah Kane's Cleansed was judged Best Foreign Language Play in 1999 by Theater Heute in Germany. Gary Mitchell won the 1999 Pearson Best Play Award for Trust. Rebecca Gilman was joint winner of the 1999 George Devine Award and won the 1999 Evening Standard Award for Most Promising Playwright for The Glory of Living.

In 1999, the Royal Court won the European theatre prize New Theatrical Realities, presented at Taormina Arte in Sicily, for its efforts in recent years in discovering and producing the work of young British dramatists.

Roy Williams and Gary Mitchell were joint winners of the George Devine Award 2000 for Most Promising Playwright for Lift Off and The Force of Change respectively. At the Barclays Theatre Awards 2000 presented by the TMA, Richard Wilson won the Best Director Award for David Gieselmann's Mr Kolpert and Jeremy Herbert won the Best Designer Award for Sarah Kane's 4.48 Psychosis. Gary Mitchell won the Evening Standard's Charles Wintour Award 2000 for Most Promising Playwright for The Force of Change. Stephen Jeffreys' I Just Stopped by to See the Man won an AT&T: On Stage Award 2000.

David Eldridge's Under the Blue Sky won the Time Out Live Award 2001 for Best New Play in the West End. Leo Butler won the George Devine Award 2001 for Most Promising Playwright for Redundant. Roy Williams won the Evening Standard's Charles Wintour Award 2001 for Most Promising Playwright for Clubland. Grae Cleugh won the 2001 Olivier Award for Most Promising Playwright for Fucking Games.

Richard Bean was joint winner of the George Devine Award 2002 for Most Promising Playwright for Under the Whaleback. Caryl Churchill won the 2002 Evening Standard Award for Best New Play for A Number. Vassily Sigarev won the 2002 Evening Standard Charles Wintour Award for Most Promising Playwright for Plasticine. Ian MacNeil won the 2002 Evening Standard Award for Best Design for A Number and Plasticine. Peter Gill won the 2002 Critics' Circle Award for Best New Play for The York Realist (English Touring Theatre). Ché Walker won the 2003 George Devine Award for Most Promising Playwright for Flesh Wound. Lucy Prebble won the 2003 Critics' Circle Award and the 2004 George Devine Award for Most Promising Playwright, and the TMA Theatre Award 2004 for Best New Play for The Sugar Syndrome.

Richard Bean won the 2005 Critics' Circle Award for Best New Play for Harvest. Laura Wade won the 2005 Critics' Circle Award for Most Promising Playwright and the 2005 Pearson Best Play Award for Breathing Corpses. The 2006 Whatsonstage Theatregoers' Choice Award for Best New Play was won by My Name is Rachel Corrie.

The 2005 Evening Standard Special Award was given to the Royal Court 'for making and changing theatrical history this last half century'.

ROYAL COURT BOOKSHOP

The Royal Court bookshop offers a range of contemporary plays and publications on the theory and practice of modern drama. The staff specialise in assisting with the selection of audition monologues and scenes. Royal Court playtexts from past and present productions cost £2.

The Bookshop is situated in the downstairs ROYAL COURT BAR.

Monday–Friday 3–10pm

Saturday 2.30–10pm

For information tel: 020 7565 5024

or email: bookshop@royalcourttheatre.com

PROGRAMME SUPPORTERS

The Royal Court (English Stage Company Ltd) receives its principal funding from Arts Council England, London. It is also supported financially by a wide range of private companies, charitable and public bodies, and earns the remainder of its income from the box office and its own trading activities.

The Genesis Foundation supports the Royal Court's work with International Playwrights.

Archival recordings of the Royal Court's Anniversary year are made possible by Francis Finlay.

The Skirball Foundation funds a Playwrights' Programme at the theatre. The Artistic Director's Chair is supported by a lead grant from The Peter Jay Sharp Foundation, contributing to the activities of the Artistic Director's office. Over the past nine years the BBC has supported the Gerald Chapman Fund for directors.

The Jerwood Charity supports new plays by new playwrights through the Jerwood New Playwrights series.

ROYAL COURT DEVELOPMENT BOARD
Tamara Ingram (Chair)
Jonathan Cameron (Vice Chair)
Timothy Burrill
Anthony Burton
Jonathan Caplan QC
Sindy Caplan
Gavin Casey FCA
Mark Crowdy
Cas Donald
Celeste Fenichel
Joseph Fiennes
Amanda Foreman
Gavin Neath
Michael Potter
Kadee Robbins
Mark Robinson
William Russell
James L Tanner

PUBLIC FUNDING
Arts Council England, London
British Council
London Challenge
Royal Borough of Kensington & Chelsea

TRUSTS AND FOUNDATIONS
The ADAPT Trust
American Friends of the Royal Court Theatre
Gerald Chapman Fund
Columbia Foundation
The Sidney & Elizabeth Corob Charitable Trust
Cowley Charitable Trust
The Dorset Foundation
The Ronald Duncan Literary Foundation
Earls Court and Olympia Charitable Trust
The Foundation for Sport and the Arts
The Foyle Foundation
Francis Finlay
The Garfield Weston Foundation
Genesis Foundation
Jerwood Charity
Lloyds TSB Foundation for England and Wales
Lynn Foundation
John Lyon's Charity

The Magowan Family Foundation
The Laura Pels Foundation
The Peggy Ramsay Foundation
The Rayne Foundation
Rose Foundation
The Royal Victoria Hall Foundation
The Peter Jay Sharp Foundation
Skirball Foundation
Wates Foundation
Michael J Zamkow & Sue E Berman Charitable Trust

50TH ANNIVERSARY PROGRAMME SPONSOR
Coutts & Co

SPONSORS
Aviva Plc
BBC
Cadogan Hotel
City Inn
Dom Pérignon
Doughty Street Chambers
dunhill
Giorgio Armani
Links of London
John Malkovich/Uncle Kimono
Pemberton Greenish
Simons Muirhead & Burton
Smythson of Bond Street
Vanity Fair
White Light

CORPORATE BENEFACTORS
Insinger de Beaufort
Merrill Lynch

BUSINESS AND MEDIA MEMBERS
AKA
Bloomsbury
Columbia Tristar Films (UK)
Digby Trout Restaurants
Grey London
The Henley Centre
Lazard
Peter Jones
Slaughter and May

PRODUCTION SYNDICATE
Anonymous
Dianne & Michael Bienes
Ms Kay Ellen Consolver
Mrs Philip Donald
John Garfield
Peter & Edna Goldstein
Richard & Robin Landsberger
Daisy Prince
Kadee Robbins
William & Hilary Russell
Kay Hartenstein Saatchi
Jon & NoraLee Sedmak
Ian & Carol Sellars

INDIVIDUAL MEMBERS
Patrons
Anonymous
Dr Bettina Bahlsen
Katie Bradford
Marcus J Burton & Dr M F Ozbilgin
Mr & Mrs Philip Donald
Tom & Simone Fenton
Daniel & Joanna Friel
John Garfield
Lady Grabiner
Charles & Elizabeth Handy
Jack & Linda Keenan
Pawel & Sarah Kisielewski
Deborah & Stephen Marquardt
Duncan Matthews QC
Jill & Paul Ruddock
Ian & Carol Sellars
Jan & Michael Topham
Richard Wilson OBE

Benefactors
Anonymous
Martha Allfrey
Amanda Attard-Manché
Varian Ayers & Gary Knisely
John & Anoushka Ayton
Mr & Mrs Gavin Casey
Sindy & Jonathan Caplan
Jeremy Conway & Nicola Van Gelder
Robyn Durie
Hugo Eddis
Joachim Fleury
Beverley Gee
Sue and Don Guiney
Sam & Caroline Haubold
Tamara Ingram

David Juxon
David Kaskell & Christopher Teano
Peter & Maria Kellner
Larry & Peggy Levy
Barbara Minto
Mr & Mrs Richard Pilosof
Elaine Potter
Anthony Simpson
Brian D Smith
Sue Stapely
Sir Robert & Lady Wilson
Nick Wheeler
Sir Mark & Lady Wrightson

Associates
Act IV
Anonymous
Jeffrey Archer
Brian Boylan
Alan Brodie
Ossi & Paul Burger
Clive & Helena Butler
Gaynor Buxton
Lady Cazalet
Carole & Neville Conrad
Margaret Cowper
Andrew Cryer
Linda & Ronald F. Daitz
Zoë Dominic
Kim Dunn
Celeste Fenichel
Charlotte & Nick Fraser
Gillian Frumkin
Sara Galbraith
Jacqueline & Jonathan Gestetner
Vivien Goodwin
David & Suzie Hyman
Mrs Ellen Josefowitz
Colette & Peter Levy
Mr Watcyn Lewis
David Marks
Nicola McFarland
Gavin & Ann Neath
Janet & Michael Orr
S. Osman
Pauline Pinder
William Poeton CBE & Barbara Poeton
Jeremy Priestley
Beverley Rider
John Ritchie
Lois Sieff OBE
Gail Steele
Will Turner
Anthony Wigram

ROYAL COURT
SLOANE SQUARE

22 September – 7 October
Jerwood Theatre Upstairs

ON INSOMNIA AND MIDNIGHT
by **Edgar Chías**

translated by **David Johnston**

direction **Hettie Macdonald**
design **Lizzie Clachan**
lighting design **Rick Fisher**
sound **Paul Arditti**
cast **Vanessa Bauche and Nicholas le Prevost**

In a big city hotel room, a man and the maid are talking. But the more they talk, the more danger they face, and neither knows where it will lead. ON INSOMNIA AND MIDNIGHT is a tale to frighten chambermaids in the night.

A Royal Court co-production with the Festival Internacional Cervantino in association with the British Council and the Centro Cultural Helénico and suppported by the Genesis Foundation.

With additional support from Anglo Mexican Foundation, Mexican Embassy London, and México Tourism Board.

INTERNATIONAL PLAYWRIGHTS: A Genesis Project

10 November – 22 December
Jerwood Theatre Downstairs

DRUNK ENOUGH TO SAY I LOVE YOU?
by **Caryl Churchill**

direction **James Macdonald**
design **Eugene Lee**
lighting design **Peter Mumford**
sound **Ian Dickinson**
music **Matthew Herbert**

Jack would do anything for Sam.
Sam would do anything.

Caryl Churchill's new play receives its world premiere at the Royal Court Theatre this autumn. Her previous plays for the Royal Court include A Number, Far Away, Blue Heart, This is a Chair and Top Girls.

Supported by an anonymous donor.

BOX OFFICE 020 7565 5000
BOOK ONLINE
www.royalcourttheatre.com

We've always been happy to be less famous than our clients

Piano/Forte

For Alice, in her eighteenth year

Characters

Abigail, *mid-twenties*
Louise, *mid-twenties, Abigail's sister*
Clifford, *mid-fifties, their father*
Ray, *late forties, Clifford's brother-in-law*
Dawn, *late twenties, Clifford's fiancée*
Juan, *late twenties, aerialist/acrobat*
Caterina, *mid-twenties, aerialist/acrobat*
Bouncers, *large men in suits*

Act One

Scene One

*Light comes up to isolate **Ray**, looking slightly awkward in a jacket and tie, like an unwilling witness at an inquest. He's an Australian in his late forties. Wiry rather than muscular. He's speaking his thoughts rather than addressing us, as if the witness has forgotten where he is.*

Ray . . . that the gun was fired to disperse the starlings? Which had roosted overlong in the old beech across from the house. That the gun was fired at the dog, to put the devoted old bitch out of her misery? That the gun was fired in anger, that the gun was fired accidentally, jarred on the cobbles of the courtyard? That the gun was complicit in murder, or harmed only the one who dropped it? Or was is fired deliberately, into a mind that yearned for it, an attempt to articulate everything in the momentary embrace . . . of nothing. All those possibilities, encompassed in one uncertain moment beyond which our lives had either changed unrecognisably, or would continue as before, an unforgiving trudge through dank mortality. The birds stayed put. They knew it wasn't meant for them. Most times, outdoors, a shot means nothing. But sometimes the sound of it implodes upon your own worst imaginings. A shot that kills has a certain echo to it, and this had none. But before the silence had enveloped it . . . there was a second shot.

Lights fade swiftly.

Scene Two

At first glance, the setting for a Gothic murder mystery. At second glance, the reception room of a small (six-bedroomed) mock-Tudor manor house on the outskirts of a Home Counties market town. The main room has retained an authentic feel. The furniture is dark oak and mahogany, the walls panelled. An impressive, heavy-set bar has been built beneath the stairs some fifty years ago. A grand piano in one corner. A wide staircase spills into the room from upstairs. Beyond a wide door a soft lime-green, metal-fitted kitchen, circa late fifties, boasts a large wooden table and an Aga. Outside, one hundred acres of subsidised farmland lazily rotates.

Abigail *is a quiet, reserved, somewhat reclusive girl in her early to mid-twenties. Her hair is tied back and she's wearing glasses. She's carefully varnishing the panelling in a far corner of the room, renewing the pale emulsion on the wall between the beams.*

Unseen, the heavy cast-iron knocker on the other side of the thick oak front door emits a shuddering series of bangs. **Abigail** *balances her brush, goes to the door, but doesn't answer it.*

Abigail   Who is it?

Louise (*off*)   Me.

Abigail   Louise?

Pause.

Louise   Abi?

Pause.

Abigail.

Another three knocks.

Abigail, will you please open the fucking door. Abigail?

Another four knocks.

Abigail   G . . . go away.

Louise   Let me in.

Abigail   I can't.

Louise   Just open the door.

Abigail   You know I c . . . an't

Louise   Abigail, it's drizzling. It's five degrees below. I've been raped.

Abigail   You've what?

Louise   On the way here. I hitched the wrong ride.

Abigail   Are you hurt?

Louise   Please, Abi?

Abigail   I'm not allowed. You know I'm not.

Louise   Jesus, he's coming up the drive . . .

Abigail   Who?

Louise   He's got a machete . . . Abi? Open the door!

Abigail   A m . . . a machete?

Louise   He's got his dick out, Abi; it's fucking enormous. For Christ's sake open the door!

Abigail   I don't b . . . I don't b . . . I don't b . . .

Louise   Oohf! No, please . . . don't. Please d . . . Argh! Oohf! Oohf! Oohf! Oohf! Abigail, for pity's sake; I've got a madman's dick up my arse!

Abigail   Well, it w . . . ouldn't be the first time.

Louise   What am I going to do, set fire to the place?

Abigail   That, either.

Louise   I'm not staying. I just want a cup of cocoa and to pick up some clothes.

Abigail   What clothes?

Louise   Jumpers.

Abigail   You haven't got any j—

Louise   Wetsuit.

Abigail   What wetsuit?

Louise   Tennis racket.

Abigail   There's n . . . othing left to steal.

Louise   I'm not going to steal anything.

Abigail   Have you got matches?

Louise   No.

Abigail   A hammer or something?

Louise   Abi, please. That was then. I'm unarmed.

Abigail   Lulu?

Louise   What?

Abigail   Please, just go away.

Louise   I know all about it, Abi. I know what's happening. I think you need me. And it's *really* cold out here.

Abigail *opens the door.* **Louise** *enters. She looks a bit like* **Abigail** — *they could be non-identical twins — but she's altogether much wilder in appearance and manner. Dressed in an eccentric, eclectic multilayered array, she appears simultaneously aimless yet passionate, clear-thinking yet drink- and narcotics-driven . . . in short, a complete liability.*

Louise   Thank you.

She strides across the room . . .

Treacherous cunt.

. . . up on to a sofa, pulls down a large family portrait and slams it over the sharp corner of the banister, splitting it in half.

Symbolic gesture. Heavy-handed. There'll be a few of those because THAT'S THE SORT OF GIRL I AM.

She goes behind the bar and serves herself a large whisky.

Three fucking days it's taken me to get here. I was in Aber-fucking-deen. And there was a rapist, if you must know. A lorry driver in Leeds. He pulls off the motorway on to the B30516 or some such dirt road to nowhere and he turns into a field and stops the engine and I thought, fuck this, but the doors are bloody locked. How about it, he says. I tell him no chance, so he pulls out a knife. A fucking great skin-yourself-a-rabbit knife. I'm thinking, what have I done to deserve this? What have I done in my life that these things keep happening to me? So he points the knife at my neck and smiling a little smile he says, 'So, do you want to suck my cock or do you want your throat cut?'

Abigail   What did you do?

Louise   Well, I'm home, aren't I?

She picks up something valuable, throws it, catches it.

Abigail   Please don't.

She puts down the valuable.

Louise   When are they due?

Abigail   Who?

Louise   When do you expect them?

Abigail   T . . . omorrow.

Louise   Super. Are you renovating the whole house or just tarting up that particular corner?

Abigail   What do you want?

Louise   A welcome'd be nice.

Abigail   Then why do you make it so imp . . . imp . . . imp . . .

Louise *toys with a vase.*

Abigail   That was Mother's. That was hers . . . please don't . . . not his. It's me that deals with it. It's me that clears it up, or b . . . uys another, or gets the men in. The things you do, you do to *me*, not him. So p . . . lease . . . for *my* sake.

Louise   Everything I do, when I'm here –

Abigail   Which is n—

Louise   – is for your sake. Abigail.

Abigail   Was it for my s . . . ake you set your bed alight?

Louise   Yes, as a matter of fact. I thought it might get you out of the house.

Abigail That's n . . . nonsense.

Louise I fell asleep. I was smoking. I was drunk.

Abigail You're lucky you weren't alone.

Louise I was alone.

Abigail Who were the n . . . aked men, then?

Louise What naked men?

Abigail The naked men I saw running across the lawn.

Louise Naked men?

Abigail They sat you in the fountain to make sure your n . . . nightdress was out and then they legged it across the tennis court.

Louise Seriously?

Abigail You don't remember?

Louise If I could remember I'd have put out the cigarette. Why haven't you mentioned this before?

Abigail I didn't know you d . . . idn't remember.

Louise Who were they?

Abigail I've seen them in the town.

Louise Well, that narrows it down.

Abigail It wasn't for my sake, thank you.

Louise You'll not leave here until it's rubble and cinder.

Abigail How are you?

Louise I'm all right. I'm in control. Everything's under control.

She tries to open the piano lid. When it won't open she slides an ornament to the edge of it.

Abigail Are you on something?

Louise Want some?

Abigail   Have you got stuff on you?

Louise   NO!

Abigail   Well, g . . . ood.

She puts the valuable back.

Louise   Have you met her?

Abigail   Who?

Louise   Don't be deliberately fucking obtuse, Abigail.

Abigail   Why are you here?

Louise   I've come to claim my inheritance.

Abigail   Well, you d . . . destroyed most of it last time.

Louise   Doesn't matter what I do with it as long as it gets *spent*. Burned to the ground. All this family deserves now, is to smoulder.

Abigail   There's no money. Except the subsidy. They p . . . ay us to grow nothing, do nothing. We had to sell the herd.

Louise   Not Molly?

Abigail   No, not Molly.

Louise   I read in the paper he bought a house in Chiswick.

Abigail   That doesn't mean we've got m . . . oney, that means we've got m . . . inus six hundred thousand. He re-mortgaged.

Louise   But you live here.

Abigail   Not for much longer, mmm . . . aybe. Not for ever.

Louise   Abigail, are we . . . *poor*?

Abigail   Well, I s . . . uppose, yes, we are.

Louise   What about the celebrity lifestyle?

Abigail   He lives it. That's w . . . here the m . . . oney goes.

Louise   Selfish fucker.

A silence.

Abigail (*quietly*)   You should g : . . . o.

Louise   I'm looking forward to it. The pair of them. Walking through the door.

Abigail   No.

Louise   No what?

Abigail   You w . . . w . . . won't be here.

Louise   I will.

Abigail   No, p . . . lease don't be here.

Louise   Nice finish. I'd swear there was a handle. I'd swear there was a door.

Ray *appears beyond the French windows with a wheelbarrow. He moves deliberately: a once-strong man rendered weaker by a dodgy heart valve.*

Louise   Is Ray still here?

Abigail   Obviously.

Louise   How is he?

Abigail *and* **Louise** *stare at each other as* **Ray** *opens the door and carries in logs.*

Ray   Logs.

Abigail   Thanks, Ray.

Louise   Hello, Uncle Ray.

Ray (*nods*)   Trouble.

Louise   You have to be nice to me. Abigail's being horrid.

Ray   *Was* nice to you. Once.

Louise   I remember.

Ray   Sprained my wrist and lost my driving licence.

Louise   But they didn't catch us.

Ray Bloody close call.

Abigail What? What are you . . . ? What did you . . . ?

Louise Is it still a secret?

Ray Yes.

Abigail What is?

Louise Sorry, Abigail. It's a secret.

Ray That dog's back legs have given up the ghost.

Abigail Poor Blanche.

Ray And Molly's calf died.

Abigail Oh.

Ray Bloody silage has gone solid, but I shot a few rats.

Louise God, it's good to be home.

Ray Half that dog's worn out and the other half's worn out dragging the worn-out half around.

Louise Don't let her suffer.

Ray Speaking of which, what sort of strife are you going to put us through this time?

Louise You love me really.

Ray Fancy a beer?

Abigail Don't let her d . . . rink.

Ray I'm having one.

Abigail It's only three o'clock.

Ray Soon be Christmas.

Louise How are you, Ray?

Ray Knackered in the mornings, knackered in the afternoons, knackered all night.

Abigail (*fondly*) Don't get him started.

Ray   Wouldn't mind if I was working.

Abigail   You w . . . work harder than any of us.

Ray   Call this work? Not what I call work. Shovel a ton of chicken shit, it's still just chicken shit. I used to be a Working Man. How's the circus?

Louise   I ran away from it.

Ray   That's original.

Louise   I fell off the trapeze. Halfway down I had a revelation.

Louise *and* **Ray** *smile, then . . .*

Both   Don't go back up.

Louise   It was startlingly vivid.

Ray   You got yourself a skill though, that's important.

Louise   Yeah, you never know when falling twenty feet into a field of mud might come in handy.

Ray   Mud's all right.

Louise   Not that suddenly. Or that incessant. Mud in your hair, mud in your tea, mud in your bed. When I signed on, I honestly thought I was going to fly. My whole life I'd dreamed of that. But it's hard up there. You need all the strength you've got just to hold on.

Ray   How's the juggling?

Louise   Never cracked it. Only one end of a scimitar you can catch –

Both   Twice.

Louise   I slept with three of the clowns, turned the fourth down, he took an overdose of Lemsip, everyone ended up hating me. So I jumped ship in Leicester, borrowed a dog, went begging. Little old lady throws a quid in my hat and the dog bit her. I did an audition for Spearmint Rhino. He said to come back that night in fancy dress. I went as a fairy. He said,

'What the fuck have you come as?' I said, 'I'm a fairy – you said fancy dress.' He said, 'I said *fantasy* dress.' Chucked me out. I had to walk home in sparkly spandex and a pair of wings.

Ray   Anyone can fail to succeed. But it takes a very special person to fail at failure.

Louise   I owe it all to you, Ray – you're my inspiration.

Ray *takes a breath.*

Louise   You all right?

Ray   I'm fucking fine. Get the fuck out of it.

Louise   Oh, sit down.

Ray   Got work to do.

Louise   Have another beer?

Ray   That's an idea.

Louise *gets them beers.*

Louise   What do you think about all this?

Ray   None of my business.

Louise   Yes it is.

Ray   I just work here.

Louise   You must have an opinion.

Ray   Nah.

Louise   Yeah.

Ray   He's fifty years old . . .

Louise   Yes, he is.

Ray   He's filthy rich.

Abigail   He isn't.

Ray   He's got a hundred acres.

Abigail   The b . . . ank has.

Ray   He's a household name.

Louise   He's a complete cunt. I mean that with no disrespect, of course. To cunts.

Ray   Either way, he can do what he likes.

Louise   She's half his age.

Ray   They're getting married. She'll catch up.

Louise   I've seen her on quiz shows. She's got the IQ of a mollusc.

Ray   She held her own in the rainforest.

Louise   I heard she had her frontal lobes enhanced with Botox.

Ray   The nation wouldn't let her leave the jungle.

Louise   The only place in a thousand years she would have found my father attractive was knee-deep in guano surrounded by a TV crew.

Ray   It was a very endearing romance.

Louise   What are they going to live on, witchetty grubs?

Ray   I hope you're not intending to misbehave.

Louise   I never *intend* anything.

Ray   So why do things happen?

Louise   I don't know. I just turn up and they do.

Ray   Clifford's been good to me.

Louise   He's a louse. One wife in the ground, one in the bin, one on the cover of *Loaded*. It astonishes me he hasn't got a couple more stuffed and mounted above the fireplace.

Abigail   Catherine's not in the b . . . in, she's in a cottage in W . . . iltshire.

Louise   How is she?

Abigail   Being l . . . ooked after.

Louise Not by him, though. Another accident he walked away from, another crime he left the scene of . . .

Ray Your father's not entirely to blame. Strong men attract weak women, like moths to a flame.

Louise He didn't burn Catherine, he just pulled her wings off. My mother, on the other hand –

Ray The brighter the flame, the more suicidal the moth.

Louise Is that all she was? Your sister, our mother – a moth?

Pause.

Ray There was something missing in Phoebe. Her way of connecting with the world was a bit faulty. Like a soldered joint gone dry somewhere out of sight. All the joy could go out of her until you gave her a bit of a shake. You know this. I saw it all the time we were growing up. Even as a nipper. Except when she played the old piano, then she'd light up the room. We'd have the entire neighbourhood standing round the parlour. She played so beautifully we all presumed that playing made her happy. We should never have pushed her into the scholarship and we should never have let her come to England. I don't blame Clifford.

Louise So, if my mother was a bipolar moth, what was Catherine? A coincidence?

Abigail Catherine's a p . . . p . . . paranoid sch . . . izophrenic.

Louise Before they met or the week after?

Ray Louise, she stabbed him with a pencil. That renders her victim status a little fuzzy at the edges.

Louise Our mother kills herself, our stepmother's virtually non-functional. I'm off the rails, and Abigail's tied to them. Your starter for ten: who's the common denominator?

Ray You're not going to sort the world out by seeing it in black and white, Lou. You've got to start colouring it in a bit. Phoebe and Catherine weren't abducted. They were dependent personalities, and Clifford gave 'em good odds. You're just furious because you're not your father's only focus of attention.

Louise Oh, you should be a psychiatrist. Office on the fifth floor; leave the window open; your patients could come in and jump straight out.

Ray Wouldn't do you any good, would it? You still have three or four lives left.

Louise Have you met her yet?

Abigail N . . .

Ray No.

Louise She's going to be a complete child, isn't she?

Ray I expect so.

Abigail Hardly, I should think.

Louise He's going to fuck her dry –

Ray Your mouth!

Louise – and throw her back to the paparazzi.

Ray Even Clifford's got a sell-by date. I reckon he's going all in.

Louise Maybe she's planning to give him a coronary.

Ray Good luck to 'em, anyway.

Louise You've lost weight.

Ray People have been telling me that for thirty years. So how can that be true?

Louise You're looking good.

Ray For someone so untrustworthy, you're a fucking awful liar.

Louise How are you, then?

Ray You don't think twice about your heart until it misses a few beats, and then you can't stop thinking about it. You wonder how it *knows* to keep going as long as it does. It's a miracle it thumps at all, let alone for ninety fucking years. Lord knows, it shouldn't be such a shock when it stops.

Louise   You look much better.

Ray   Sunbed.

Louise   Seriously?

Ray   Arse off.

Louise   Why do you stay here, Ray?

Ray   Who else'd have me?

Louise   Your wife would. Your kids would.

Ray   I send 'em what I can.

Louise   You do it for Abigail and I'm grateful, but I'm sad for you, Ray. You should be home.

Ray   I better go and close up.

Abigail   Come back later.

Ray   No. I got a bit of stew on.

Louise   Come back for a drink.

Ray   I got stuff to do.

Louise   Come back for a *drink*.

Ray   All right, you're on.

Louise   Ray?

Ray   What?

Louise   I love you.

Ray   Ta.

Louise   Ray?

Ray   What?

Louise   Abigail loves you.

Ray   That's good.

Louise   And, Ray? Your wife loves you and your kids love you and we all love you.

Ray   Whatever.

He leaves.

Abigail   If you can be so nice, why are you always so vile?

Louise   I guess I'm a conundrum. I'm a bit of a conundrum, I suppose.

Abigail *opens a drawer and takes out some money, then opens her purse and empties it. Thrusts the cash at* **Louise**.

Louise   And you wonder why I'm alienated.

Abigail   I'm just trying to avoid the in . . . evitable conflict.

Louise   All I want to do is wish them the best for a happy and fruitful marriage. I'm going to make them a card. I'm going to glue some macaroni on a bit of cardboard and spray it gold.

Abigail   He d . . . d . . . doesn't w . . . want you here.

Louise   He loved me once. I remember it distinctly. I was wearing bunny-rabbit slippers.

Abigail   Why can't you just g . . . et a job and live a n . . . ormal life like the rest of us?

Louise   Normal?

Abigail   You know what I m . . . ean.

Louise   Well, sadly, in your case, no.

Abigail   I mean be *nice*.

Louise   Oh. For a moment there I thought you meant go to the shops, or go see a movie, or walk down the drive, you know; normal as in *leave the house*, for instance? Because when was the last time you did that?

Abigail   Never m—

Louise   When was the last time you stepped out of the
house, Abigail?

Abigail   Please change the subject, p . . . p—

Louise   I thought the subject was 'being normal', so I was
just attempting to define –

Abigail   . . . lease!

Louise   And why's the piano locked?

Pause.

Abigail   What?

Louise   The piano's locked.

Abigail   So w . . . hat?

Louise   Why's the piano *locked*?

Abigail   I d—

Louise   Why's the fucking *piano* locked?

Abigail   You c . . . can't c . . . You can't come here like this
and do this.

Louise   Where's the key?

Abigail   I d(on't) . . . I d(on't) . . . I'd(on't)—

Louise   He *locked* the piano?

Abigail   No, he d—

Louise   How dare he? How fucking *dare* he?

Abigail   Please. D . . . on't make a fuss. It's not important.

Ray *returns, takes off his boots.*

Ray   There's a car coming up the fields. It's your father's.

Abigail   No, that's tomorrow.

Ray   Yesterday it was tomorrow. Today, evidently, it's today.

Abigail   But he . . . I haven't . . .

Ray   Abi, put the kettle on.

Abigail   She isn't meant to b . . . e here.

Ray   Do you intend to confront him straight away or will you lull him into a false sense of security with an overwhelming display of filial devotion?

Louise   Cordelia got a bum rap, you know.

Ray *has produced a medication box – modest, but indicative of a daily routine.*

Louise   I don't need drugs.

Ray   That's the only time you want them, isn't it? When you don't need them.

Louise   I don't want them and I don't need them.

Ray   They're not for you.

He gives **Abigail** *some tablets.*

Ray   Warm the pot. Four tea bags.

Abigail   Ray, I c . . . I c . . . I c . . .

Ray   Abigail. Take a breath. You can handle this.

Abigail   Make her b . . . ehave.

She returns to the kitchen.

Louise   Since when?

Ray   Since a few months ago. Look, couldn't you make yourself scarce for five minutes? This is hard for her too; let her get her bearings.

Louise   *Leave It to Abi*, by Ingrid Blitton.

Ray   You what?

Louise   All those books, I read them all. Whatever happened to all those Brave Girls, Ray? Who did they grow into?

A car pulls up outside.

Ray It'd be easier on her if you weren't here.

Louise It'd be easier on all of us. It'd be easier on me, frankly.

Ray Please, Louise. For Abigail.

After a second, she runs upstairs.

Louise I shall listen from the landing. That's what young heroines do.

Ray (*to himself*) Jesus fuck me backwards.

He finishes his drink, turns to get another as **Abigail** *comes in from the kitchen.*

Abigail Where is she?

Ray Upstairs.

Abigail Don't let him s . . . I opened the door, I wasn't to open the d . . .

She has a childlike little panic attack.

Ray Abigail. You can handle this.

They hear the key in the lock. **Abigail** *moves into a corner and* **Clifford** *enters. A tall and distinguished man around fifty years old. Dressed in conservative Armani. Self-confident and undeniably charming. A cross between Alan Clark and Melvyn Bragg. He ushers in* **Dawn**, *twenty-five: a curvaceous English rose with expensively streaked blonde hair and an immaculately flattering wardrobe.*

Clifford Wait.

Dawn What?

Clifford Tradition.

He lifts her over the threshold.

Dawn Careful. You'll get a hernia.

Clifford I have it on good authority there's a high incidence of hernia amongst honeymooning males.

Dawn   Overweight brides?

Clifford   Blow jobs apparently.

Dawn   Oh well, that's a challenge.

Clifford   I should hope so.

They kiss.

Ray   Welcome home.

Clifford (*surprised*)   Ray.

Dawn   Oh. Hi.

Clifford   Sorry.

Ray   How do you do.

Clifford   Christ. And Abi. Ray and Abi. This is Abigail.

Dawn   Hi.

Clifford   And this is Dawn.

Dawn   Hi.

Abigail   P . . . leased to meet you.

Clifford   And this is the house.

Dawn   Oh! Oh my gosh.

Clifford   Home sweet home.

Dawn   It's . . .

Clifford   Well . . .

Dawn   It's extraordinary.

Ray   Kettle's on.

Abigail   I'll go and –

Ray   No. I'll go and. Say hello to your dad.

He leaves.

Abigail   Hello.

Clifford   How are you?

Abigail   I'm fine. Everything's f—

Dawn   Fine?

Abigail   Fine, thank you.

Clifford   I need a drink. Do you need a drink?

Dawn   Oh no, just . . . a cup of tea would be great.

Abigail   Daddy, there's a p—

Clifford   Sit yourself down. I've some very special single malts here, if my brother-in-law's not polished 'em off.

Dawn   No, just a cup of tea.

Abigail   Theres' a bit of a p—

Clifford   There's a what?

Abigail   A bit of a p—

Clifford   Problem?

Abigail   . . . problem. It's n . . . ot just the four of us.

Clifford   This is twenty-five years old.

Dawn   Oh, all right then. I'll keep you company.

Clifford   Not just the what?

Dawn   Although, could I have both?

Clifford   Ray! Fetch her a cup of tea or we'll never hear the end of it.

Dawn   God, I love it here, It's really . . .

Abigail   Beautiful?

Dawn   Yes.

Clifford   How *is* Ray?

Abigail   He's all right.

Clifford   Keeping an eye on you?

Abigail   Yes.

Clifford   What's wrong with the dog?

Abigail   Blanche?

Clifford   She was dragging herself down the drive.

Abigail   Her legs.

Dawn   Poor thing.

Clifford   Hardly humane to let her suffer like that, is it?

Abigail   But it's B . . . lanche.

Louise   Thought I heard voices.

She appears down the stairs. She's taken her top off.

You must be Dawn. Hello, Daddy. (*To* **Dawn**.) It's *really* nice to meet you. (*To* **Clifford**.) Welcome home. (*To* **Dawn**.) Well, and you, of course. Welcome home to both of you. What?

Abigail, *terrified of the consequences, turns her back and sits.*

Clifford   This is um . . .

Dawn   Louise.

Louise   Good guess. I can't say I've heard a lot about you because my father barely speaks to me but of course I know who you are. I've followed your career in the newsagents and I thought you were terrific in the tank of fish guts and I've always thought you had a lovely face. And you have. Your face is really lovely. Is it cold in here or is it me?

Clifford   Go back upstairs.

Louise   Don't be so rude. I want you to feel at home here. And I want you to know that even though, technically, you *are* my stepmother, that doesn't bother me a bit and I have no intention of treating you like one. It's my sincere hope that we can relate to each other more like sisters. You can be the younger sister because . . . well, because you probably *are*.

Clifford   Make yourself decent or I'll throw you out the door.

Louise   Daddy, please. I'm going out of my way to be welcoming here.

Dawn   It's a pleasure to meet you.

Louise   It certainly is.

Dawn   However. Never front-on. Forty-five degrees to camera, feet parallel and pull your shoulders back.

Louise   Better?

Clifford   Christ.

Dawn   That's much better, yes.

Louise   Thank you.

Clifford   Why the fuck are you encouraging her?

Louise   Luscious Louise is your Sunday Sizzler this week. Her ambition is to marry a man with a Grade II listed manor house, and very high cholesterol.

Abigail *curls up in a corner.*

Clifford   You're upsetting your sister, as usual.

Louise   I've come to apologise.

Clifford   What for?

Louise   In advance.

Clifford   Get dressed.

Louise   Where's your sense of humour?

Clifford   We've had your little laugh, and we didn't, now get dressed.

Louise   No thanks. Just to fill you in, Dawn: at this point every muscle in his body is aching to grab me by the arm and throw me out the front door. But because you're here and I'm only half dressed, he can't see a way of doing it without appearing ungentlemanly. I have put him in an existential quandary. He cannot defend his pride without damaging his dignity. He is in a furious state of impotence. A very volatile state. And there you sit, a witness to whatever masculinity eventually manifests itself. I for one can't *wait* to see what happens.

A pause. **Clifford** *gives* **Dawn** *her drink. Sits down opposite them.*

Louise   He is, of course, a triumph of education over breeding. His baser instincts have always been channelled most effectively into the accumulation of wealth and respect. The balls of his id are firmly grasped in the fist of his ego, and the head of his ego is firmly inserted up his super-anus.

Ray *comes in from the kitchen.*

Ray   Tea's up.

He looks at the tableau.

Cake or biscuits?

He puts down the tray. Finds a rugby shirt on a peg beneath the stairs and throws it at **Louise**. *Heads outside.*

Ray   I'll be in the small barn if you need me.

He disappears out of the French windows.

Clifford   So, to what do we owe the displeasure of your company?

Louise   Nice reversal. Oratorical. I like what you did there.

Dawn   May I say something?

Louise   Yes, you may.

Dawn   I think your father's a remarkable man.

Louise   He has been much *remarked* upon, particularly as to how, in spite of lacking the initiative to run a measly hundred acres, he succeeded in becoming the first of a long line of politicians who, with a ceaseless dedication to corrupt and/or scandalous behaviour, managed to decimate the Tory Party and render it permanently unelectable.

Dawn   He's had an extraordinary career.

Louise Far more extraordinary that the likes of Clark, Aitkin and Archer managed to out-disgrace him. Now, of course, resignation is deemed sufficient a penance for lying to one's wife, the House, and under oath. But Daddy was the first to discover that political disgrace can be transformed into personal aggrandisement, by way of television light entertainment. Let a couple of celebrities take the piss out of you on BBC2 and some of that celebrity will eventually rub off, like lard on a pig.

Dawn Would you mind if I poured?

Louise Down the nearest drain if you're that flexible.

Clifford That's enough, please.

Louise My father blazed a tawdry trail of infamy until his persona was burnished bright by his self-effacing wit and the inestimable charm of the rogue survivor. Now he's a perennial panellist, restaurant critic, visitor to Greek islands, rainforests and, here's his big trade secret, *always available*. If they can't get anyone else, they know they can get Clifford.

Dawn He's very popular.

Louise He's an ugly, disintegrating gargoyle on the minor celebrity guttering of the besmirched, deconsecrated cathedral of British culture. For some bizarre reason I'm the only one I know who finds him hard to like.

Clifford Louise joined a circus.

Louise Our mother killed herself.

Dawn I know.

Clifford Would you like to see the farm?

Dawn Yes. I'd love to.

Clifford You'll need some boots.

He exits.

Louise I hope you don't think I'm trying to compete or anything. The tits were more an abject gesture of defeat, before we begin.

Dawn   Begin what?

Louise   . . . whatever.

Dawn   I know all about your mother.

Louise   No no no no no. You *think* you do.

Clifford *returns with boots.*

Clifford   You have to realise that Louise has always been hell-bent on self-destruction. When she was born she wrapped the umbilical round her neck in a spectacular attempt to live her life and end it simultaneously.

Louise   Whereas Abigail emerged wearing tap shoes and practising scales.

Clifford   I'd appreciate it if you weren't here when we get back. I don't expect you to have either the maturity or the good grace to deal with the next few days, so we both know it would be best if you left.

He takes out his wallet, gives her the contents.

Here.

Louise   Oh, soon be Christmas.

She takes the money. **Clifford** *ushers* **Dawn** *out of the French windows.*

Clifford   Watch your step.

Dawn   What's that smell?

Louise   Depends which way the wind's blowing.

They leave.

Louise   Come out of there or I'll put a match to the upholstery.

Abigail *comes out.* **Louise** *picks up her drugs.*

Louise   You don't need any of this crap.

Abigail   Yes I do. If I d . . . on't everything goes . . . p . . . pear-shaped.

Louise   There's nothing wrong with you that a trip to
Tesco's and a good fuck wouldn't cure.

Abigail   I'm mildly p . . . aranoid. I have free-floating
anxiety and d—

Louise   This is bullshit.

Abigail   . . . d . . . epressive tendencies. I do.

Louise   Well, that's nothing. I have multiple-personality
disorder. One of me's an impulsive maniac with dubious circus
skills and the other's a terminally shy agoraphobic who used to
play the piano but lives in virtual silence. Oh no. That's you.

Abigail *laughs a little.*

Louise   We've got to get you off these.

Abigail   Where's D . . . addy?

Louise   He's showing her the pigshit.

Abigail   Why do you d . . . islike him so much?

Louise   When he got found out, he kidnapped contrition
and stripped her naked on the moral high ground. Glorified
himself. A man who knows what's good, what's bad, but also
knows what's good for him, wink, wink, superior grin, and they
fucking fell for it.

Abigail   He talks and p . . . eople listen.

Louise   Why is that? Why do my words disappear into thin
air, while his words fall to earth with the weight of prophecy?
Because every frosty Home Counties bitch and her greedy
blackguard husband *worship* him. They laud his non-PC
pontifications and applaud his puerile derring-dos because
they no longer have a viable political party to express their
vile, self-serving instincts, that's why.

Abigail   If you're staying for the wedding, I don't expect you
to help but could you at least not hinder?

Louise   Is there a band?

Abigail   There's . . . Elton John. If he can make it.

Louise *sits in silence, fuming.*

Louise   Ever wondered why he never sold this place? Why you have to live here still? To satisfy in him some vague sense of stoic superiority, of having risen above such a thing as feelings, on to a plane of emotional logistics –

Abigail   I b . . . arely understand a word you say.

Louise   Our mother died here. You shouldn't live here. He should have let us go.

Abigail   Go then. Or are you s . . . s . . . staying or what?

Louise   When you think of Mother, what do you think? Apart from the piano, what else?

Abigail   Apart from the starlings?

Louise   And the music – what else?

Abigail   A boiled egg.

Louise   Her sole contribution to the culinary arts.

Abigail   The perfect boiled egg.

Louise   And painted, at Easter. And hidden.

Abigail   The lawn, damp. The dawn.

Louise   She must have loved us then, those mornings, don't you think?

Abigail   Are you staying or going? What are you going to do?

Louise   Remember when she took us to see the puppets? And they started off very small and each new scene they got bigger and bigger until the last one was full size and she was a pianist. And she played and played until her hands came unattached, and her head rose off and she fell apart. Until the music stopped and she came back together again?

Abigail *has returned to her varnishing.*

Abigail   I don't remember.

Louise *dives into her backpack and pulls out a plastic toy piano. She plonks away on it, an inept tune emerging.* **Abigail** *stares at her. The lights fade.*

Scene Three

Night. **Ray**, **Louise** *and* **Abigail** *are sitting in the near-dark. An open dictionary in* **Abigail**'s *lap.*

Ray   A wilderness of monkeys.

Louise   A what?

Ray   A wilderness.

Louise   That's not true.

Ray   A business of ferrets.

Louise   A business?

Abigail   A busy-ness.

Ray   A mob of kangaroos. A clutter of cats.

Abigail *(relishing)*   A trembling of finches.

Ray   A parliament of rooks.

Louise   A bucket of toads.

Ray   You can't just make 'em up.

Louise   Why not? A snuggle of kittens. A slaughter of piglets.

Ray   Shut up and learn something.

Abigail   A bouquet of pheasants. An exalt . . . ation . . .

Louise   An exaltation?

Ray/Abigail   – of larks.

A silence.

Louise   Play something.

Abigail *wraps herself tighter in a thin duvet.*

Ray   Leave her be.

Louise   I could break the lock. I'm a dab hand at locks. Remember the mink farm?

Ray   Drop it, Louise.

Louise   It was us; Ray and me.

Abigail   It w . . . You b . . . ?!

Louise   Off they scattered, like the final reel of some Disney shit.

Ray   To decimate the entire chicken population of Buckinghamshire.

Louise   Abigail thinks we're irresponsible.

Ray   You *are* irresponsible. I was misguided.

Louise   Go home, Aussie.

Ray   I can't go home.

Louise   Anyone can.

Both   'Well I'm HOME, ain't I?'

Abigail *looks perturbed.*

Ray   Robert Mitchum. On a chat show.

Abigail (*to* **Louise**)   But you said that was you.

Louise   I lied.

Ray   I consider myself an exile. Most I ever hoped for was an honest day's work, good shoes for the kids. In my dreams, maybe a forest. Get that extra bit of land, put your name on it, plant a couple of hundred trees. That's one more thing's never going to happen now. I can live with that. A dream's just a dream, but a good pair of trainers . . .

Louise   I'm sure they've got trainers, Ray.

Ray Yes, but it'll be the wrong label on 'em, eh? And I know I'm not worth half of what your father sends 'em. I'm a fucking charity case.

Louise Ray, you're *ill*.

Ray I'm a fucking invalid.

Louise Yes, you are.

Ray Hyphenate that and what have you got?

Louise Then work harder, Ray! Get a spade and spread that pigshit and when you feel a bit rough, dig harder. Give us one good day, then we'll throw your corpse on the back of the tractor and remember you fondly down the Black Horse.

Ray You can laugh.

Louise I feel the same way Vicky feels. I'd like you to fly back to Melbourne and sit on your arse in the backyard and drink beer until you're eighty. Maybe you could nick the odd pair of trainers. Oh, and maybe you could shag your wife a couple of times a week.

Ray Well, as it happens, no, I couldn't.

Louise Oh.

Ray If it makes my heart beat faster, I'm not allowed it.

Louise Well, put her on top and watch *Neighbours*.

Ray Thanks for the advice. I feel much better.

Louise I love you, Ray.

Ray So you said.

Louise Vicky loves you.

Ray Rumour has it.

Louise Everyone loves you.

Ray That's all right then.

Louise So GO HOME, you Aussie shitbag.

Dawn *comes down the stairs in pyjamas.*

Louise   Look out, it's the stepmother. You clean the fireplace, I'll look for a pumpkin.

Dawn   I was wondering if I could get a glass of water?

Abigail   I'll go.

Dawn   It's all right.

Abigail   No, I'll g . . . o.

Ray   Have a drink.

Dawn   No, it's late.

Ray   Have a malt.

Dawn   Well . . . do you mind?

Louise   Join the Thursday Club.

Dawn   Oh, is that a thing?

Louise   Yes, if it's Thursday.

Ray   Whereas if it's Friday . . .

Louise   It'd be the Friday Club.

Dawn   Oh. Well . . . start as I mean to go on, or whatever. Thank you. I will. If I'm not intruding.

They give **Dawn** *her drink.*

Thank you. Oh, thank you. I can't get over the house. It's spooky.

Pause.

Louise   Boo.

Dawn   I'm aware there are issues, between you and your father. I'm well aware. I can understand how hard it is, for you to see him objectively. I mean, he's your father and it's hard. I never got on with mine, and then I hit Page Three, I thought, well, that'll be that. But suddenly I was his pride and joy. All I'm trying to say is . . . he's really very proud of you.

Louise   He said that?

Dawn   In so many words.

Louise   How many?

Dawn   Well . . . one or two.

Louise   Not an entire sentence, then.

Dawn   Anyway, I know there are issues and I hope I don't exacerbate them. Make them worse, that means. Maybe in time I could even . . . bring you closer together, I don't know.

Ray   Welcome to the family.

Dawn   Oh, thank you. Thank you. I hope I will be, manage to be, eventually. Thank you. I could never replace your mother, I know.

Louise   You could, though.

Dawn   Could I?

Louise   If I dug her up first, you'd fit nicely.

Ray   Louise.

Louise   What?

Ray   Don't . . . overstep the mark.

Louise   Is there one?

Ray   Well, there's common decency.

Louise   Which was entirely my point. Respecting the dead and so forth.

Ray   Drop it, Lulu.

Louise   Abi found her.

Abigail   L . . . L . . .

Ray   Leave it.

Louise   She went out to the barn first thing to see the piglets.

Ray   We don't want to hear it; neither does she.

Louise   They wrapped us in blankets, they drove us to Grandma's. Our mother's name was Phoebe. She was Ray's sister.

Dawn   I know. I know all this.

She idly picks up the dictionary.

Ray   Not tonight, Lulu. I don't want to go there.

Louise   You won't *leave* though, will you, Ray? You'll stand at the window and stare at the rain. You'll go behind the bar and pour another malt. You'll work yourself stupid, stumble back to the cottage and sleep for twelve hours, but you won't *leave*.

Ray   A murder of crows.

Louise   That doesn't surprise me.

Abigail   A p . . . itying of doves.

Louise   A suddenness of relatives.

Dawn   A murmuration.

Silence.

Louise   What?

Ray   Um . . .

Dawn   A murmuration of starlings.

Abigail *has gone very still.* **Louise** *puts her arm around her.*

Ray   We don't –

Dawn   What?

Abigail *gets up and goes to the kitchen.*

Louise   Abi?

Abigail   I'm coming b . . . ack.

Dawn   What?

Ray   Abigail doesn't like the starlings.

Dawn   Oh. Sorry.

Pause.

You know what I *don't* want? I don't want 'Here Comes the
Bride', even if Elton's playing it. It's cheesy. I want that tune
from *Robin Hood*. (*She sings a snatch of Bryan Adams, 'I Do It For
You'.*) More modern, more romantic. First impressions, I don't
think we'll be living here, on the whole. The Chiswick house
is nice. We're going to knock a lot of walls out.

Louise   A vacuum of glamour models?

Dawn   Look. I'm sorry about your mother.

Louise   Thank you.

Dawn   And I mean to say, I don't want to tread on anyone's
feet. I don't want to live here. In fact, what I don't quite
understand, considering, is why any of you do.

Ray   House was built by Clifford's great-grandfather. You
don't close down the family manse because some neurotic
Australian girl ends her life in one of the sheds.

Louise   Some highly strung . . .

Ray   Willow-thin . . .

Louise   . . . absent-minded . . .

Ray   . . . beautiful girl.

Louise   That wouldn't be the English way.

Ray   Boarding school for the girls was the English way.

Louise   And a more resilient wife. Resilient as in brittle,
insensitive bitch, of course.

Dawn   Well, I think you'll find I'm none of those, once you
get to know me.

Louise   I have no intention of getting to know you.

She goes to the kitchen.

Dawn   Fighting a losing battle, aren't I?

Ray *pours her another.*

Dawn   Oh, I shouldn't.

Ray   My old man had a motto. 'Don't drink. Don't smoke. Don't fornicate. Die anyway.'

Dawn   Oh, chip off the old block. Make the most of it, that's what I say.

She downs it in one.

Ray   Abi couldn't cope with boarding school, so she came back home.

Dawn   They say when there's a trauma you have to confront the trauma.

Ray   Yeah, well . . . she confronted it. Then spent ten years of her life trying to forget it again. It's taken her a long time to get this far.

Dawn   Oh well, I suppose I'll get the hang of it.

Louise *comes back, dragging* **Abigail** *by the hand like a little sister.* **Abigail***'s got a glass of milk.* **Louise** *sits her down, negotiates the milk, and wraps the both of them in the duvet.*

Louise   Abigail says can we talk about something trivial.

Dawn   How did you end up here, Ray?

Louise   Ray's here because there's things he'd like to say, but he hasn't got the nerve to say them.

Ray   I'm here because Clifford's the only man stupid enough to employ me.

Louise   (Guilt.)

Ray   I've a duff heart.

Louise   (Broken.)

Ray   I came over to lay a few ghosts.

Louise   But they won't lie down.

Ray No, Lulu. They won't walk into the room.

Louise Ray settled for silence, and the silence settled all around him.

Ray *drinks again.* **Dawn** *holds out her glass.* **Louise** *pulls* **Abigail***'s hand out of the duvet and examines it, tenderly.*

Louise Abigail used to play the piano, but the piano's locked. She could be playing anywhere. The Philharmonic. Fact. The Purcell Room. And once upon a time there was a piano. But the piano's locked.

Dawn Well, nothing wrong with a bit of peace and quiet.

Louise Disturbing though, silence, when it's undisturbed.

Dawn If I'm to be honest, and you must excuse me for saying so, I don't think there's a healthy atmosphere in this house.

Louise Our mother used to play.

Abigail *withdraws her hand.*

Louise There. I said it. She taught us both. I was very bad at it and Abigail was very good.

Pause.

Dawn I'll go back to bed, then.

She goes to the foot of the stairs.

If you knew me, you'd know I'm a perfectly nice person.

Louise A simplicity?

Dawn A what?

Louise Of glamour models?

Dawn I don't think so, no.

Louise Well, a thingy, anyway.

Dawn Well, as a matter of fact, a decency.

She goes to bed.

Louise   Ray?

He's asleep. **Abigail** *emerges.*

Louise   Ray?

Abigail   Don't wake him. He barely sleeps. He'll only rest an hour or two.

Louise   Which of us is it that's afraid of the starlings?

Abigail   Me.

Louise   That's right. I forgot.

Abigail   You always wanted to be up there with them. In the m . . .

Louise   Murmuration. Eye of the storm. Have they been this year?

Abigail   Not yet.

Louise   Ray'll get in the truck, he'll go get Old Edwin, who'll fly his hawk. They can't hurt you.

Abigail   But they can. Obviously they could. All those things that can't hurt us – all of them can.

Louise   I wish you'd get out of here.

Abigail   W . . . hy?

Louise   Well, beyond the obvious; Ray's never going home, is he? So long as you're here.

Abigail (*quietly*)   None of your b—

Louise   No, nothing ever is. Does he know?

Abigail   What?

Louise   That you feel the same way he does?

Abigail   Ab . . . out what?

Louise   One another.

Abigail   I don't see w . . . You w . . . alk in here –

Louise   You're not lovers, I know that.

Abigail   Of course we're n . . . n . . .

Louise   Are you?

Abigail   No!

Louise   I thought not. I think you and Ray are the only two people I know who could live out here and fall in love and never even mention it. When you drink together you sit at opposite ends of the kitchen, don't you? He falls asleep with his head on the table; you put a blanket round him and tiptoe to bed, don't you?

Abigail (*silent*)   W . . .

Louise   Do you leave the door ajar?

Abigail   He sleeps in the cottage.

Louise   I know. But I don't understand.

Abigail   Why does it m . . . ystify you that life can be lived in ways you can't imagine? You find the most ordinary behaviour p . . . erverse.

Louise   Why don't you tell him?

Abigail   Tell him w . . . ?

Louise   If you want him, have him.

Abigail   Well, th . . . at's your answer to everything.

Louise   Take him.

Abigail   W . . . ant it; take it.

Louise   I would.

Abigail   I know you would. But he wouldn't.

Louise   Look.

Abigail   What?

Louise   I found the key.

Abigail *looks.*

Abigail   Where?

Louise   In that old key box in the barn. There's a key for everything in there.

She goes to the piano and unlocks it with the small key.

Abigail   Don't.

Louise *opens the piano and begins to play one half of a children's duet for four hands. She plays unexceptionally badly.*

Abigail   It's late. You'll wake him.

Louise   Play, then. I can't play. Play the Ravel.

Abigail *shakes her head.* **Louise** *staggers through a few bars of 'Pavanne pour une enfante défunte', bumming the sixth chord.*

Abigail   You'll w . . . ake everyone up.

Louise   Play some Chopin.

Abigail   Nnnn . . .

Louise   Just a little one.

Abigail   No.

Louise   Abigail, I can pound away on this and wake the house or you can play a prelude and everything will feel better and we can all sleep soundly. I found the *key* for you.

Abigail   I don't want to play.

Louise   Yes you do, I know you do.

Abigail   I d—

Louise   You'd sit here all day. This was where you'd sit.

Abigail   That was Mother.

Louise   So were the starlings. Play the Ravel. For me.

Abigail *goes to the piano.* **Louise** *stands,* **Abigail** *sits. Then she closes the piano and locks it.*

Louise   Abi . . . !

Abigail   He didn't lock the piano.

Louise   Don't defend him.

Abigail   He d . . . He d . . . He d . . .

Louise   Well then, who did?

Abigail   I did.

Louise   *You* did?

Abigail   Y . . . yes.

Louise   But –

Abigail   So, p . . . please.

Louise   But why?

Abigail (*shrugs*)   Just had enough.

Louise   How long since you played?

Abigail   I don't –

Louise   How long ago?

Abigail   The last time you listened. A few t . . . imes after that. I can't remember.

Louise   Why, Abi?

Abigail   Oh, w . . . hat do you care?

Louise   Why did you lock the piano!?

Abigail   Because if the p . . . if the p . . . if the piano's locked I can't p . . . I can't p . . . I can't play the piano!

Pause.

Louise   Well, obviously.

She opens the piano.

Now. Play.

Abigail   You p . . .

Louise   I can't play.

Abigail   Yes, you can.

Louise   Only with stickers on the keys. Never like you. No one plays like you. Even she never played like you.

Abigail   Life's very s . . . imple. You Wake Up in the Morning, there are Things to Do. You d . . . o them. Well, I do them. *You* send postcards from P . . . rague.

Louise   Do I?

Abigail   We read your p . . . ostcards, we finish the day, we open a b . . . ottle of wine. If we want m . . . m . . . m . . . If I want to hear m . . .

Louise   Music.

Abigail   Music! (*Pause.*) I turn on the radio.

Louise   That's hardly the same.

Abigail   It's all I can c—

Louise   This is unbearable.

Abigail   No, it's Bearable. It's very Bearable. It's you that finds it un-Bearable, so you want to make it un-Bearable for everyone else. When you're not here, we do fine.

Louise, *upset, pounds on the piano, playing Rachmaninov spectacularly badly, then slams down the lid.* **Ray** *wakes.*

Ray   Jesus Christ.

Louise *rises from the piano and pinches* **Abigail***.*

Louise   Play me something.

Abigail   Ow! Don't.

Louise   Play me something.

Abigail   No.

Louise *pinches her again. Then again and again, different parts of the body.* **Abigail** *tries to retreat.* **Louise** *tries a Chinese burn, then pulls her hair; she is incessant and a little vicious.*

Abigail   Ow. Ow!

Ray   Pack it in, Louise.

Louise   She wants to play the piano, but I have to persuade her.

Abigail   Stop it. Ow!

Ray   Lay off! Jesus Christ!

Abigail *runs to* **Ray** *and he embraces her. The solidity of the embrace makes* **Louise** *collapse like a discarded doll.*

Ray   You know what? Life's a lot easier when it's just the two of us.

Louise   Only wanted to hear some fucking Chopin.

Ray   She don't play no more.

Louise   Since when?

Ray   Since you stopped being here.

Louise   She doesn't need me here to play.

Ray   Maybe she needed you here to *listen*.

Abigail   No. When Mother played it was entirely her. The notes were her; she'd lose herself and b . . . ecome a thousand notes. When I play, all I can hear are the bad notes, and the slipped pedal, the wrong length of silence. Too much reverb, not enough attack . . . a stream of notes n . . . ot quite good enough, not quite what I meant . . . So there's all this m . . . music inside me and all this imperfect sound around me, and I feel so imperfect, and full of *her* . . . Last time I p . . . layed I looked down at my hands . . . and it wasn't me.

Ray   You've Phoebe's hands.

Abigail   I've little hands. Hers were bigger.

Louise   Hers were the size yours are now.

She takes **Abigail** *by the hand and leads her to the piano.* **Abigail** *eventually opens it, and plays the Ravel.* **Ray** *listens.* **Louise** *listens.*

Ray   I've missed this. What's is it?

Abigail   'Pavanne pour une enfante d . . . éfunte'.

Louise   'Dance for a Dead Child'.

Then, eventually . . .

That's enough. That's enough. THAT'S ENOUGH!

Blackout.

Scene Four

The afternoon of the wedding. Beyond the windows, a huge marquee has been erected. Unseen caterers have commandeered the kitchen. **Abigail** *is fixing a corsage to her bridesmaid's dress. A Spanish waiter and a Spanish waitress trip down the stairs, arguing.*

Juan   *¡Está perfectamente seguro!* [It's perfectly safe!]

Caterina   *¿Pero no ves que este edificio tiene más de cien años?* [But the building's more than a hundred years old?]

Juan   *Bueno, mujer, no te pongas así.* [Don't be such a woman.]

Caterina   *¡Ahora tienes responsabilidades, chaval! Buenas tardes, señorita.* [You have responsibilities now, you big child. Good afternoon, Miss.]

Abigail   Er, what are you doing upstairs?

Juan   *¿Perdón?*

Abigail   Do you speak English?

Juan   *Sí.*

Abigail   Well, *do* you?

Caterina   *Sí.*

Abigail   Then w . . . *ould* you?

Juan   *Sí, sí.* (*To* **Caterina**.) *¿Qué te parece para otro trio?* [What about her for another threesome?]

Abigail So wh . . . at were you doing up*stairs*?

Juan *kisses her.*

Juan *¡Riquísima!* [Cutey!]

He backflips over the sofa.

Caterina *¡Dios!* (*To* **Abigail**.) *No le hagas caso.*[Ignore him.] (*To* **Juan**.) *¡Fantasma cabrón! ¿Es que tienes que ligar con todas las inglesas palíduchas con las que te tropiezas?* [Arrogant bastard! Do you have to flirt with every pasty English girl you trip over?]

She does a cartwheel and they both adjust their clothing and disappear towards the marquee. **Louise** *comes down the stairs.*

Louise Nice frock. What's wrong?

Abigail One of the w . . . aiters kissed me. Half of them are Sp . . . Spanish. They don't understand a word you say. They just grin at you. Then they do acrob . . .

Louise Acrobatics?

Abigail . . . Yes!

Louise You're imagining things.

Abigail It's all going p . . . ear-shaped.

Louise Relax. It's all first class. Bouncers down the drive, hand-picked paparazzi, profiteroles . . . it's a jolly splendid day.

Abigail Just tell me you'll b . . . e good, then I can relax.

Louise I'll be good.

Abigail Good.

Louise Is it *Hello!* or *OK!*?

Abigail *Hello!* They g . . . azumped *OK!* I've got to speak to the band.

Louise I've spoken to them.

Abigail She doesn't want 'Here Comes the Bride'.

Louise   She wants the theme from *Robin Hood*. I've sorted it . . . !

Abigail *goes off in the direction of the garden.* **Louise** *opens champagne.* **Clifford** *comes downstairs, half dressed in his morning suit. During the following he finishes dressing.*

Clifford   It didn't work.

Louise   What didn't?

Clifford   The limo people phoned *my* people for confirmation. It was not forthcoming. Have you any other little surprises?

Louise   I'm sorry?

Clifford   An artificial fox trail through the marquee, perhaps? Nitroglycerine in the cake?

Louise   I've no idea what you're talking about.

Clifford   You ordered a limousine, to pick up in Tidworth.

Louise   Oh, that limousine.

Clifford   You needn't have bothered. Catherine refused to get in it.

Louise   Well, she falls way short of being a just cause, but she'd have made a hell of an impediment.

Clifford   Your stepmother spent five years of her life in an institution as a direct result of your behaviour. Your incessant undermining of her mental health. Your absurd aggression. Your undisguised *contempt*.

Louise   You're blaming *me*?

Clifford   You drove her insane.

Louise   Oh, please. She was a founder life member of the Priory before I even met her. She was addicted to everything it's humanly possible to be addicted to. She fell off a catwalk in Milan.

Clifford   She had a sensitive disposition which failed to weather your incessant assaults. As did our marriage.

Louise   You abandoned her!

Clifford   She asked for a divorce!

Louise   And you're blaming *me*?

Clifford   I can't discuss this now.

Louise   For *your* behaviour?

Clifford   I am laying blame, yes, firmly, yes, on your abject *irresponsibility*!

Louise   Since I was knee-high I have been blamed for everything: broken ornaments, the price of chocolate biscuits, my own personality. It has become your habit to blame me for existing, like throwing a blanket over a sparrow. Well, Catherine wasn't my fault. She was an anorexic nymphomaniac who you only married because she came thirty-fourth in the *Daily Mail*'s 'Hundred Sexiest Women of 1988'.

Clifford   You burned her underwear.

Louise   Not specifically *her* underwear.

Clifford   You put a dead rabbit in her bed.

Louise   I burned her clothes in the back seat of your limousine, ergo, it was a message for you. I put the rabbit in *your* bed; she found it.

Clifford   It was *our* bed.

Louise   IT WAS MY MOTHER'S BED!

Clifford   Let me tell you something about your mother's bed. She had sole possession of it our entire married life.

Louise   Good for her.

Clifford   I remember we slept together in my room at Trinity, when you were conceived. And again the weekend we came up here to inform your grandmother she was going to be one. On that sofa. Me rather insistent, she rather reticent.

Louise   Too much information, thank you.

Clifford   And Abigail came along, so there must have been other times but I can't for the life of me remember them.

Louise   Is this conversation entirely appropriate?

Clifford *looks at his watch, sits.*

Clifford   I'd been invited back to give the Howarth Lecture, and that evening, on the banks of the Cam, the sun setting, I saw your mother play a concert. She played with such a concentrated passion that I couldn't take my eyes off her. I took her a glass of champagne, and walked her through the colleges and conjured her, God knows how, into my old rooms. She seemed shy, but otherwise willing enough.

Louise   This *is* too much information.

Clifford   It was only the next morning, as the Sunday bells echoed soberly around the quad, and she lay there, silent and unresponsive, then dressed with an awkward, prosaic sadness, that I realised she was utterly ashamed. And, as it turned out, pregnant.

Louise   I always suspected I was inconsequentially conceived.

Clifford   We embarked upon a virtually celibate marriage. When it came to sex your mother was crippled with shame. And that was the cause of it, if you ask me.

Louise   Of what?

Clifford   Her illness, her misery. Your birth nearly killed her.

Louise   Well, it wasn't deliberate.

Clifford   She was in abject denial of your existence. Lived her life in denial of her own. She could hardly bear to live in the body God gave her. She lived only in her own tentative perception of the world, and in her music.

Louise   None of us exist for you but for how you see us. You keep us in your head like toys in a closet. Tiny Tears escapes, dispatches herself in the woodshed, and you go buy yourself a Barbie to undress.

Clifford   You hounded Catherine until she couldn't take a teacup from a saucer.

Louise   I liked Catherine. The way she put her hair up, and took it down, and put it up again. With pencils. The way she spoke in non sequiturs, of things entirely other than those being discussed . . .

Clifford   I sometimes wonder . . .

Louise   I even liked her underwear, which I'm sure you did.

Clifford   I wonder if, consciously or otherwise –

Louise   Oh, consciously, let's presume.

Clifford   – you were trying to push Catherine into the woodshed too. It occurs to me a second suicide might have gratified you.

Pause.

Louise   Only yours.

Clifford   Innocence is no refuge for you, young lady. Not a single thing we do or say is meaningless. There is purpose in the smallest gesture, the quietest utterance, let alone your brand of extravagance and fury.

Louise   You've started to talk in real life the way you talk on *Question Time.*

Clifford   How much money do you want to just fuck off?

*Enter **Ray**, in his morning dress.*

Ray   How do I look?

Louise   Like an Australian farmhand at a posh wedding.

Ray   Thank you.

Clifford   She's all yours.

Louise   Are you giving me away?

Clifford   Ray's agreed to sit on you, if necessary, while the ceremony takes place.

Louise   You fucking traitor.

Clifford   Family loyalty may be an alien concept to you, but some of us rather appreciate the tradition. Thank you, Ray.

His mobile phone rings.

Yes. Good. Good!

He leaves.

Louise   He's been getting all confessional. Apparently my mother was a frigid headcase.

Ray   Don't go there, Lu. Don't insult Phoebe. I'm one of the few friends you've got.

Louise   Is that what we are, Ray? Friends?

Ray   For Christ's sake, girl, I'm doing my best here. I'm hanging on by my bloody fingernails. You don't like what's going on so piss off out of here and leave 'em to it!

He pours champagne. It foams over his hand.

Gaah. Stupid fucking stuff.

Louise   I think I'll stay.

Ray   All that's going to happen is you're going to get drunk and hurl a couple of insults and then one of those hired gorillas is going to drive you to the station and throw you on a train.

The Spanish waiter and waitress come in and speak in Spanish.

Caterina   *Alguien me ha pedidio* 'sparkling water'. [Someone asked me for sparkling water.]

Juan   *Agua con gas.* [Sparkling water.]

Caterina   *¿Es que parezco una* 'waitress'? [Do I look like a waitress?]

Juan   *Sí.*

Caterina   *¡Qué gilipollez!* [Stupid idea.]

Ray Excuse me . . .

Juan   *¡Hey, inglesita!*

Caterina   *¡Ah, por fin!* [Ah, there she is!]

Louise   *¡Habéis venido!* [You made it!]

Juan   *Con el disfraz perfecto, ¿no?* [The perfect disguise, no?]

Louise   *¡Estáis fantásticos!* [You look great!]

Juan   *¿Este es amigo o enemigo?* [Is this a friend or foe?]

Louise   *Por ahora amigo. Cuánto de enemigo . . . . no lo sé.*
[Erstwhile friend. How much of a foe, I don't know.]

Caterina   *Mi amiga preciosa. ¡Cuánto te he echado de menos!* [Lulu,
my beautiful friend. I've missed you!]

Louise   *Y yo a ti.* [Oh, so have I.]

Juan   *Y yo a ti.* [And so have l.]

Caterina   *Y él a ti pero no tanto como yo.* [And so has he, but
not as much as me.]

Behind **Ray**'s *back,* **Juan** *and* **Caterina** *fondle* **Louise***.*

Juan   *Este culo sabrosón.* [Your beautiful arse.]

Caterina   *Estas tetas tan apetecibles.* [Your lovely tits.]

Ray   Jesus, Louise; do you have to be so familiar with the
staff?

Abigail *comes in. Her corsage has fallen off.*

Abigail   The p . . . ews are filling up. And I've lost my little
pageboy.

Louise   *No llaméis mucho la atención. Quedáos en la cocina fumando
con los demás.* [Keep a low profile. Hang out with the rest of
them, smoking in the kitchen.]

Juan   *¡La vida es un show!* [Life is a performance!]

Caterina   This sister of you is beautiful. *Hasta luego.* [See you
later.]

Caterina *disappears.* **Juan** *kisses* **Louise** *tenderly.*

Juan   *Te he echado de menos.* [I've missed you.]

Louise   *No deberías. Ya te avisé.* [Well, I told you not to.]

Juan   *Eres muy linda.* [You're beautiful.]

Louise   *Ya lo sé. ¡Vamos!* [I know. Vamoose.]

Juan   *Vete.* [Vamoose.]

Louise   *¡Vete!* [Vamoose]

Juan *follows* **Caterina** *into the kitchen.* **Abigail** *tends to her corsage.*

Ray   Since when did you speak Spanish?

Louise   Since last summer in Spain.

Ray   What were you doing in Spain?

Louise   Topless escapology.

Ray   That's just an average Friday night outside Wetherspoons for you, isn't it?

Louise   Bit of high-wire snogging . . .

Ray   Yeh, but since when were you in catering?

Dawn *comes downstairs in full bridal wear.*

Louise   Ooh look, a virgin.

Dawn   Well?

Louise   What?

Dawn   How do I look?

Abigail   You look b . . . eautiful.

Louise   Have you got the full basque on under that?

Dawn   Oh well, something old. (*She flickers a wicked grin.*)

Louise   My father, isn't it?

Dawn   Something new.

Louise   His hair.

Dawn   Sugar. I haven't borrowed anything.

Louise *throws a pair of Doc Martens at her.*

Abigail   Hanky?

Dawn   Thanks.

Ray   Something blue?

Louise   Her CV.

Dawn   I'm wearing something blue.

*She winks at **Ray**; they laugh.*

Clifford (*off*)   Abigail . . .

Dawn   Don't let him in!

Ray   Don't come in, mate.

Clifford   Abigail!

Louise   Yes?

Abigail   Don't!

Ray   Stop it.

Dawn   Don't let him come in!

Ray   Clifford mate, don't . . .

Louise *pushes **Ray** away from the French windows.*

Louise   Whatever you do, don't come in!

Clifford   Why not? What the fuck are you up to?

*He pushes past **Louise**.*

Dawn   Don't!

Clifford   Oh, f . . . (*Shields his eyes.*) Sorry.

Dawn   That's really bad luck!

Clifford   Sorry. I'm –

Louise   I told you not to come in.

Dawn   That's got us off to a really bad start.

Clifford   I'm *sorry*.

Louise   That's what happens when there's all this . . . familial distrust about.

Clifford   Would you –

Dawn   You've spoiled it now.

Clifford   I didn't see you. I didn't see anything.

Ray   Wait in the study.

Dawn   Jesus, Clifford, you can be a stupid pig sometimes.

She goes into the next room.

Louise   You've got about ten minutes to pull out.

Clifford   Why don't you just shut your fucking mouth?

Louise   I've been racking my brains for a way to sabotage this but it's been a complete waste of time. Please marry her. She's going to make your life a misery!

Clifford   You barely know her.

Louise   Why on earth do you think she's doing this? You think she finds your sad little paunch *endearing*? Your no doubt chemically enabled erection faintly stimulating? Your entirely narcissistic verbiage *entertaining*? I don't think so. Though she's scarcely creative enough to embody a cliché, I think she wants not you, dear Father, but one half of everything you have so far accumulated. I think in the back of her mind the divorce is proceeding very nicely.

Clifford   You will eventually learn that the pursuit of emotional independence is a lacklustre exercise that leads men to a barren stoicism and women to poverty or spinsterhood. We are what we *possess*. And, however unpalatable you may find it, if Dawn and I wish to possess one another, that's the best imaginable basis for a good marriage.

Louise   You're such a romantic.

Clifford   And possession, try as you may to overload the word with negative connotation, is in fact the cornerstone of civilisation.

Louise   Listening to you is like watching the *Titanic* plough through a starless night.

Ray   Clifford, the Minister's looking this way.

Clifford   Are people seated?

Ray   No going back now, mate.

Clifford   Abigail, go and round up the bridesmaids. The pageboy's in the pond.

Abigail *goes.* **Ray** *straightens the carnation in* **Clifford**'s *lapel.*

Clifford   Thanks. I'm relying on you.

Ray   She'll behave.

Louise   Judas.

Clifford   Right then. Into the breach . . .

Louise   No comment necessary.

Clifford   Ray, I um . . .

Ray   No need, mate.

Clifford   When Phoebe died I thought I'd never love again, and in my haste to render that untrue, I made a terrible mistake with Catherine. I realise now what I loved in her was what I recognised of Phoebe, the same . . .

Ray   All right, Clifford.

Clifford   A certain . . . dislocation. Implicit in them both.

Ray   Some other time, eh.

Clifford   I know you both think Dawn is rather young, and rather brazen, but let me tell you something: Dawn is strong. And she is not easily moulded to any man's presumptions or desires. To tell the truth, yes, she gives me a run for my money. But for reasons both obvious and not worth trying to convince you of, I love her. That's one lifetime, three loves. Judge me how you may; I can live with that.

He leaves.

Louise Apparently, once you got to know him, Fred West was a bit of a charmer.

Ray You want a drink?

Louise Don't you want to watch the service?

Ray I have my orders. I can see enough from here.

Louise How does the bride look? Is she blushing?

Ray Can't see her.

Louise I went to a wedding in Spain. An equestrian dwarf and a ballerina.

Ray I bet they made a lovely couple.

Louise Not really. I'd shagged both of them, and neither of them made a lovely couple.

The band plays the opening bars of the wedding march.

Ray Here she comes.

The band segues into the theme tune from Robin Hood *(the TV series).* **Ray** *looks at* **Louise**, *who shrugs.*

Ray Nice one.

Louise Thank you.

Under the music a dense whispering sound starts to grow subliminally.

Ray You know what I was thinking? I was thinking we ought to think about ostriches.

Louise Ostriches?

Ray Could be the saving of us.

Juan *and* **Caterina** *run in from the kitchen.*

Juan   *¿Ahora, Lulu?* [Now, Lulu?]

Louise   *No. Esperad hasta los* 'I do'*s*'. [No, wait until the 'I do's'.]

Juan   *Vale.* [OK.]

Caterina   *¡Ah, la novia está guapísima!* [Oh, the bride looks lovely.]

Louise   *La novia es un demonio,* gold-digging cow. [The bride's an evil, gold-digging cow.]

Ray   How come you're so familiar with the catering staff?

Louise   I'm sociable.

Ray   I don't believe you.

Louise   It can't just happen, Ray. *I won't let it.*

Suddenly the sunlight from the French windows dims. The whispering sound becomes an unbound rustling, a flurry, which dies as the sunlight is restored, leaving behind the odd cry of surprise.

Caterina   *¿Que ha sido eso?* [What was that?]

Ray   It can't be.

Louise   Of course it can.

Ray *and* **Louise** *go to the windows.*

Louise   Where are they?

Ray   Behind the house. Look at the congregation.

Louise   Look at their faces.

Caterina   *¿Pero, qué pasa?* [What's happening?]

Juan   *Ni idea.* [I've no idea.]

Ray   Would you bloody believe it?

Louise   Their timing was always pretty nifty, Ray.

Juan   *¿Qué está pasando?* [What's happening?]

Another flurry of starlings.

Louise   *¡Ahora!* [Now!]

Juan   *¿Ahora?* [Now?]

Louise   *Ahora es el momento apropiado.* [Now might be the right time.]

Juan   *¡Sí! ¡Ahora, Caterina!*

Caterina   *Sí.*

Juan and **Caterina** *strip off their uniforms and get naked.*

Ray   What the fuck are you up to?

Louise   Nothing.

Ray   Who are these people?

Louise   Met 'em at a festival in Barcelona.

Juan   *¡Vivan Los Furiosos!*

Caterina   *¡Vivan!*

They put on red noses.

Louise   Their *Cabaret de Sade* was a *cause célèbre*.

Ray   Jesus, Louise . . .

Louise   You're either for me or against me, Ray, when it comes right down to it.

A wave of starlings swoops past the French windows, and away. Sounds of female alarm and male laughter from outside. The band wavers.

Ray   Bloody hell.

Louise   Hello, starlings.

Ray   Here comes Abi.

Louise   Unnatural acts beget ungrateful nature, Ray. Or some such Shakespearean bollocks . . .

Juan and **Caterina** *have strapped on large dildos and transformed themselves into obscene, rather alarming clowns.*

Caterina/Juan   Da daah!

Louise   You know what I love about the Spanish, Ray?

Ray   What?

Louise   They're not fucking English.

Abigail *comes belting back in from outside.*

Abigail   Starlings! Ray! The starlings! (*Hyperventilating.*)
Thousands ofhm . . . thousands ofhm . . .

Another swoop from the starlings. **Abigail** *screams and hides under the
piano.*

Ray   You're all right, Abi.

Abigail   Make them go away!!

Ray   They won't roost near the house. Not with all those
people.

Caterina   *¿Qué son todos estos pájaros?* [What are all those
birds?]

Louise   They come once a year.

Juan   See; all the little birdies.

Ray   Would you put your clothes back on, please?

Louise   Now's the moment. Do your worst! *¡A por ellos!*

Juan   *¡Sí! ¡Sí!*

Caterina   With birds. OK.

Both   *¡Vivan Los Furiosos!*

Juan *runs upstairs,* **Caterina** *into the kitchen.*

Ray   What the fuck is going on?

Louise   What's the date, Ray?

Ray   The what?

Louise   What's the DATE today? Look at your invitation.

He takes it out of his pocket.

Ray   Oh, Christ.

Louise   . . . just cause or impediment!

Ray   I didn't notice.

Louise   No one did. But someone fucking should have!

Another swoop from the starlings. **Abigail** *screams.*

Abigail   Go away! Go away! Go away!

Ray   It's all right, Abi – you're safe.

He slumps on the sofa with his drink.

Abigail   Please, Ray, make them go *away*.

Ray   We'll let 'em settle, then we'll fly the hawk.

Abigail   *Don't* let them settle.

Ray   It's only birds, sweetheart.

The sound of gathering starlings grows louder.

Louise   It's her anniversary, Ray. He booked his fucking wedding and he didn't even notice.

Ray*'s face has gone blank.*

Ray   Of course, it's tougher than chicken, your ostrich. More like steak.

Caterina *comes out of the kitchen with clown pies. Singing a punked-up Spanish version of the theme from* Robin Hood: Prince of Thieves, *she tears out of the French windows. There's another swoop of starlings.*

Abigail   Close the w . . . Lulu, the w . . . !

Louise *runs across and slams the windows closed.*

Louise   Mother would play until they settled. Why don't you play?

Ray   It's a vicious bird, though.

Louise   Play for us, Abi. Play!

Ray   You've got to stay on the right side of it. What do you think, Lou?

Another swoop of starlings sends **Abigail** *to the piano, where she covers herself with a blanket and plays brilliant Rachmaninov very loudly.*

Lights change on the forestage, revealing **Clifford** *and possibly the Minister.* **Dawn** *takes her place beside him. The sound of starlings swooping.* **Dawn** *ducks and loses her veil.*

Dawn   Bloody Ada.

Clifford   Ignore them.

Dawn   It's like that film. I hate that film.

Clifford   Ladies and gentlemen, there's nothing to be afraid of. This happens every year, around this time. They're harmless.

Juan *bungees from an upstairs balcony and flies above them.* **Caterina** *runs on, whacks* **Dawn** *with a pie, and is lifted into the air by* **Juan***. They both sing the theme from* Robin Hood, *competing with the starlings and the Rachmaninov and the sounds of surprise and outrage from the crowd.* **Dawn** *screams and runs off.*

Clifford   Who the fuck are you?

Caterina *drops her second pie on him.*

Clifford   This is a private function! You have no right to . . . Shit! Bloody hell!

He flees. In the house, **Dawn** *appears through the window, howling and covered in custard.*

Louise/Abigail   Window!

Ray *runs and closes the window.*

Dawn   My special day!

Louise   It's not your day, you ignorant tart!

Dawn *howls and runs upstairs. Starlings swirl in the sky beyond as* **Juan** *lifts* **Caterina** *and they perform an aerial sexual pantomime, fucking and sucking each other.* **Clifford** *appears through the window, knocking* **Ray** *backwards.*

Louise   You know what day it is? YOU KNOW WHAT
FUCKING DAY IT IS?

Clifford *physically attacks* **Louise**. **Ray** *closes the door, then tries to
stop* **Clifford**. *Birds crash into the window.* **Juan**, *aided and abetted
by* **Caterina**, *ejaculates copiously over his audience.*

Blackout.

Act Two

Scene One

A few hours later. Dusk. **Abigail** *sits playing Chopin. Outside, the starlings roost in the trees and we hear the sporadic sounds of departure from the remaining guests.* **Ray** *comes in with a shotgun which he lays down before going to his usual place at the bar. He's got a black eye.*

Ray They're roosting in the beech. I was going to fire a couple of shots, but there's police and security down the drive. I could cause a riot.

Abigail *pauses in her playing.*

Abigail She's got a bottle of Château Margaux in her hand.

Ray She wouldn't.

Abigail Nineteen f . . . ifty-four.

Ray Not the fifty-four.

Abigail Listen.

The distant smash of a bottle from below.

Ray Wasn't a fifty-four. She'd open a fifty-four and drink it, but she wouldn't smash a fifty-four.

Abigail Should we let her out?

Ray No, we should let her cool down.

Abigail Are there any g . . . uests left?

Ray There's a few, like lost cows on a roundabout. Town centre's full of bemused caterers looking for the bus stop. Play. It's nice.

Abigail *resumes playing.* **Ray** *listens until two* **Bouncers** *in black suits with earpieces enter from the French windows. Each holds, at arm's length, one of the Spanish acrobats, who are both covered with the remains of the dessert buffet. They are arguing: there seems to be some dispute as* *to whether or not, during the simulated sex,* **Juan** *inadvertently buggered* **Caterina**. **Abigail** *closes the piano.*

Caterina   *Te he dicho que no cien veces. Cien veces te he dicho que no y tú tomas ventaja. No me puedo creer que tengas tan poca profesionalismo, eres un cerdo.* [I've told you no a hundred times, a hundred times I've told you no, and you take professional advantage, which is completely unprofessional; you are a pig.]

Juan   *Yo nunca haría algo así. Tú hablas de profesionalismo, yo soy un profesional. Como la capa de un pino. Yo nunca hago eso. Soy inmaculada.* [I never did this. You say professional, I am professional. I never do this. I am immaculate.]

Caterina   *Eres un cerdo. ¡Ya me advírtió mi madre!* [You are a pig. My mother warned me about you!]

One of the **Bouncers** *opens the front door and is greeted by a volley of flash photography. He closes the door. Both* **Bouncers** *get a simultaneous message through their earpieces. They dump their Spaniards on the sofa and retire to the doors, where they stand with their backs to us.*

Juan   *Nos han hecho esperar horas y horas.* [They have made us wait for hours on end.] The dessert is very cold. Would possible for some coffee, *por favor*?

Caterina   *Me quiero ir a casa.* [I want to go home.]

Ray   What's wrong with her?

Juan   We enter the marquee . . . we *simulate* the sex, you see . . .

Caterina   That is what is said, but is not what you do!

Juan   . . . This is as normal but big woman in hat, she grab at me. My foot slipped in the, this . . .

Ray   Trifle.

Abigail (*simultaneously*)   Ch . . . arlotte Russe.

Ray   Whatever.

Juan   Whatever this is, and I inadvertently achieved penetration.

Caterina   *¡Sí!*

Juan   Momentarily.

Caterina   Animal.

Juan   This is not company policy.

Ray   Glad to hear it.

Juan   Unless an intimate relationship already exist.

Caterina   Which it does not!

Juan   Which once it did and again recently also.

Caterina   Which for much longer it may not! I don't love you. You are a promiscuous pig.

Ray   One way to earn a living.

Juan   Please, our friend Louise . . .

Caterina   You friend!

Juan   Where is she, please?

Ray   So is this what she's been doing all year?

Abigail   What?

Ray   Having sex in public.

Juan   *Sí.*

Caterina   But extemporarily never!

Juan   And never in England!

Ray   Why not?

Juan   Too much policeman at the back. And also, since your Graham Norton –

Caterina   Too much participation of the audience.

Juan   But most places is for actual, *sí.*

Abigail   Couldn't you just p . . . retend?

Caterina   Fake is unreal, OK. Everyone can tell. You get in position; he pretends his penis is a foot long. Is ridiculous.

Abigail   It's p . . . ornography.

Ray   One more question.

Juan   *¿Sí?*

Ray   Why are your dildoes so much smaller than life?

He grins. **Caterina** *laughs.* **Juan** *does not. An awkward pause.*

Juan   The dildoes are a technical device, not an aesthetic one.

Caterina   It's a Spanish thing.

Juan   You never complained.

Caterina   *Me duele el culo, cerdo.* [My arse hurts, pig.]

Ray *chuckles.*

Juan   Please. Where is Louise?

Caterina   You little whore.

Ray   She's in the cellar. I'll go and get her.

Abigail *resumes playing.* **Ray** *goes under the stairs.*

Caterina   Oh, I love that. What is that?

Abigail   Chopin.

Caterina   So romantic.

Ray (*to* **Louise**, *down the stairs*)   You gonna behave?

Louise (*off*)   'ck off.

Caterina   I would love, you know what I would love? To make love, right there, in front of the audience. But is illegal. Unless is er . . . dialect? a what you say . . . contextual?

Abigail   A d . . . dialectic?

Caterina   *Sí.* So then is legal, so we do *de Sade*, so instead of making love I am *raped*, six times a night. I scream for an hour, but I don't get arrested. You play beautifully.

Abigail   Thank you.

Caterina   On Monday we tour. It is . . .

Juan   . . . Wolverhampton.

Caterina   We kidnap you, plant you in the audience, the eager volunteer.

Abigail   The what?

Caterina   You play the piano, get naked, no more English.

Abigail   N . . . no, thank you.

Juan   *Deja de ligar.* [Stop flirting.]

Caterina   But she's so much more beautiful, no?

Louise *appears scowling and stomping until she sees* **Juan** *and* **Caterina***, then brightens up incredibly and kisses them.*

Louise   *¡Queridos camaradas!* Thank you! That was inspired. That was better than Norwich. You are shameless and honest and I love you.

Caterina   I love you, too. Talk to her now.

Juan   We have to talk.

Louise   Do we?

Caterina   Tell her now.

Juan   I need to say that I, that we, that Caterina . . .

Caterina   That I am pregnant.

Juan   So.

Caterina   So, is no to be any more, this. All of us. You and him. No more.

Juan   No, is not *appropriate*.

Caterina   Appropriate! You are not appropriate. With him.

Louise   But I . . . I thought we were . . . .

Juan   We love you, *sí*, but now is life. One life, and us.

Louise   But you can't just . . .

Caterina   But we must. Is over now.

Louise   But what about me?

Suddenly the **Bouncers** *get a message through their earpieces and come and collect their Spaniards.*

Caterina   *¡Ay!*

Ray   Hey. Steady on.

They march them towards the front door.

Juan   *¡Vivan Los Furiosos!*

Caterina   *¡Vivan!*

Abigail   Where are you t . . . aking them?

Juan   No harm will befall us.

Caterina   I miss you, already. Play for us.

Abigail *plays some Bizet.*

Caterina   Life is a performance! *¡Vivan Los Furiosos!*

Both   *¡Vivan!*

Caterina *is bundled out.* **Juan** *escapes.*

Juan   Lulu!

Louise   Don't touch me.

Juan   You are always my favourite English.

He reaches to kiss her, she moves her head. A pause. **Juan** *turns to* **Abigail**.

Juan   Tell your sister I love her. And this is how much.

He sweeps **Abigail** *up and kisses her passionately.*

Juan   Goodbye.

He leaves, followed by his **Bouncer**.

Abigail   I think he s . . . till likes you.

Louise   Fuck off.

Ray   I wouldn't take it to heart, Louise.

Louise   None of your business.

Ray   I can't believe you finally made an emotional investment in someone and you chose a Spanish acrobat.

Louise   FUCK OFF!

She goes outside.

Abigail   Two.

Ray   What?

Abigail   B . . . oth of them, I think.

Ray   You think so? Serves her right, then.

Something disturbs the starlings.

Abigail   I n . . . eed to practise.

She plays a few notes of Chopin. Has difficulty. Repeats the notes awkwardly, and again, and again. **Clifford** *comes down the stairs.*

Clifford   Do you have to pound away on that thing? How is it out there? Are we rid of the photographers?

Ray   They keep pushing them down the drive. Like trying to keep eels in a bucket.

Abigail *resumes.*

Clifford   Not now, Abigail.

Abigail   The S . . . paniards have been arrested.

Clifford   Is that all? I ordered them shot. Dawn's just about pulled herself together. We're going to drive straight to the airport in the morning and fly to Antigua. Abigail, please!

Abigail   I have to p . . . ractise.

Clifford   Now?

Abigail   YES!

Clifford *is taken aback.*

Ray   She'll give it a rest when the hawk arrives. Ed's on his way with the hawk.

Abigail *resumes.*

Clifford   It's a damage limitation exercise, really. I've got my people on to it. I'm owed a few favours. It's give and take with most of these fellers. Once they've brought you down, of course, you're no further use, and I'm good copy. I think they'll see sense. Anyway, I've got my, um . . . for Christ's sake, Abigail, can we have one moment's peace and quiet, thank you!

He abruptly closes the lid and **Abigail** *bows her head.*

Clifford   The three of you have turned this place into a bloody asylum.

Ray   With respect, mate, it was you that did that when you fucked off and left us here.

Clifford   I'm very grateful to you, Ray, but you're entirely free to leave.

Ray   Who'd look after Abi?

Clifford   She's perfectly capable. Aren't you, sweetheart?

Ray   You haven't the first idea, which is why I'm staying put.

Clifford   That doesn't make you a healer, Ray. It makes you an enabler.

Louise *appears.*

Louise   That poor bloody dog, Ray. Hello, Daddy.

Clifford   So, are you entirely satisfied?

Ray   She's very ashamed of herself. She's feeling positively contrite.

Clifford   Who were those people?

Louise   Friends.

Clifford   That's the best you can do for friends, is it?

Louise   Apparently so.

She opens the piano lid for **Abigail**, *who plays.*

Louise   Listen.

Clifford   I'm listening.

Louise   It's Chopin.

Clifford   Whatever. I'm sitting here wondering what on earth I ever did to deserve all this.

Louise   Listen to the music.

Clifford (*closes his eyes*)   I've had enough bloody music to last me a lifetime.

Louise *lifts the shotgun and now points it at* **Clifford**. **Abigail** *hesitates.*

Louise   Daddy?

Abigail *stops playing.* **Clifford** *opens his eyes.*

Clifford   The thing above all other things that renders you ultimately ineffectual is your quaint reliance on cliché.

Ray   Jesus, Lou . . . you've won the day, now put that down and stop being a complete cunt.

Clifford   Is this wilful behaviour, or merely some inadvertent improvisation to round off the afternoon?

Louise   Which would you prefer?

Clifford   On balance, wilful.

Louise   That's brave.

Clifford   Not at all. I can't believe you actually intend to shoot me but, considering your legendary lack of control, I can quite easily imagine *getting shot*.

Abigail *resumes playing.*

Louise   What do you think I *intend*?

Clifford   I presume, having provoked as much anger as possible – Abigail – you're now attempting to scare the shit out of me.

Louise   The fear's gratifying but incidental. I am attempting to evoke a sense of ennui, a pause in the passage of time that might be filled with a sobering sense . . . of mortality.

Clifford   Mine, I suppose?

Louise   Well, considering which way the thin end is pointing, yes. Yours.

Clifford   And then what?

Louise   Oh, I don't know. I'm often accused of knowing exactly what I'm doing. It's always presumed I've some sort of outcome in mind. I never have. Others make decisions, I just *do* things. That's my charm.

Clifford   Ray. Take the fucking thing off her, would you?

Ray   She's not going to shoot anyone.

Louise   How do you know?

Ray   Well, it's not going to be me, in any case. I've had enough of both of you. I've got a sick animal to see to.

Abigail (*stops playing*)   Blanche?

Ray   She needs looking after. Edwin'll get here soon, get that hawk up, get some peace and quiet.

He heads outside.

Clifford   Ray . . . !

Ray turns, smiles.

Ray   It's not loaded.

He leaves.

Louise   Yes it is.

Abigail *resumes.*

Clifford   Abigail . . .

Louise   Leave Abigail alone.

Clifford   I presume this is all my fault?

Louise   What do you mean?

Clifford   All dubious acts on your part are accompanied by the apportioning of blame on someone else. More often than not, your victim. This trait you share with muggers, six-year-olds and terrorists. So I'm presuming this is something I have in some way inspired.

Louise   Er. Well. Yes.

Clifford   Abigail, please.

Abigail *stops playing.*

Clifford *stands.*

Louise   Don't stand up. Sit down.

Clifford *sits.*

Clifford   I remember, on the worst day of all our lives, when this house had become the labyrinth of a nightmare, I wandered into this room and it was full of police. How few police it takes to fill a room. And I remember your voice from upstairs. Your cry. Of sorrow? No. Of *accusation*.

Louise   How did she pull the trigger?

Clifford   Clear as a bell. How did she *pull* the *trigger*?

Louise   Legitimate question.

Clifford   Extraordinary question, for a nine-year-old.

Louise   I thought you'd done it.

Clifford   No. That's what you wanted *everybody else* to think.

Louise   And was I wrong?

Clifford   She used the cue-rest from the snooker table.

Louise   That's why I got the giggles at the inquest. It was like a game of Cluedo.

Clifford   Neither I nor you, against all evidence to the contrary, are to blame. Even your mother, if you'd let her rest in peace, was blameless.

Louise   Neither you nor my mother ever used the back stairs. They were always our domain.

Abigail *resumes playing.*

Louise   One night we heard you whispering, talking to her, quietly. We sat in the dark to listen. The starlings were roosting – they'd been here for days – so I couldn't hear the words, but I could hear the tone which, for once, was tender and compassionate. I was used to hearing shards of anger and twisted syllables of sarcasm. I was surprised at the reassuring words. Entranced by them. So we sat on the stairs and listened.

Abigail *stops playing.*

Louise   The panels of the door had warped and gaps had formed, been puttied over, the putty dried, then picked with our persuasive little fingers, slivered away until there were handy spyholes in the door. I tucked my knees into my chest, and peered through. She was sitting at the table in that way she used to sit. Forearms beneath the tabletop, resting on her thighs, her shoulders forwards, chin level, eyes unblinking. Like an automata, when you haven't got the right money to put in. You were sitting behind her, one hand on the back of her chair, the other resting on the table. Your lips at her ear. You spoke earnestly; urging her, I hoped, to happiness. Then you placed your hand against her palm. Her hand closed and you took your hand away. Your hand was empty. Hers was not. Lipstick, was my first thought. A little gift. You left her. We waited, but she didn't move. Eventually, we got up. Our little legs had gone to sleep. Crept upstairs so as not to make a noise. I imagine she sat there for half an hour or so, listening to those birds she thought were in her head and she thought would never leave it. The little something in her hand. Maybe she tried to think of some reason not to use it.

Abigail *plays vaguely, disjointed.*

Clifford   You imagined this.

Louise   No. It's a memory, though for years it remained an imagining. I once asked Dr Kasden how she distinguished between a genuine history and a false memory. She said she didn't bother to distinguish because, whatever the case, *the treatment was the same.*

Abigail *stops.*

Clifford   I'm sure you've raked over the ashes of your childhood for some inappropriate touch to justify your fury, but sadly, I never obliged. So now you pluck an ember of some conversation overheard and half remembered, and fan it to life with what? The memory of a what? A shotgun shell?

Abigail *plays.*

Clifford   A thing you just admitted you didn't even *see*.

Louise   Don't try to make it me.

Clifford   You said yourself –

Louise   Would you please be silent?

Clifford   It's a fabrication!

Louise   Silence, then.

Abigail *stops playing.*

Louise   Not you, cherub. Him.

Abigail *plays slowly, stutteringly.*

Louise   I heard nothing. I heard what I heard. Saw nothing, but saw what I saw.

Abigail *stops playing.*

Louise   I may or may not shoot you, but I won't debate. This isn't a discussion. This is *you* knowing what I know. So now you can deny it if you like, if you can live with it in my eyes. Denial or contrition? Make up your mind before you speak.

A silence. **Dawn** *comes downstairs.* **Abigail** *plays the* Robin Hood *theme.*

Louise   Ah, 'tis Maid Marian.

Dawn   No, it effing isn't.

Louise   Nay, 'tis Dawn. She enters Sherwood fleet of foot, spilling the light of day and future days across the tatty leather chaise of your sordid yesterdays.

Abigail *stops playing.*

Dawn   Is that loaded? Because, you know, accidents happen.

Clifford   Go upstairs.

Dawn   Most gun-related fatalities take place in the home, between family members.

Louise   Welcome home.

Clifford   Wait for me upstairs.

Dawn   Is it or isn't it?

Clifford   I'd rather not find out, so get the fuck upstairs, you stupid bloody woman.

Dawn *goes upstairs.*

Louise   Nice one.

Clifford   I'm not going to allow you to ruin the rest of my life.

Louise   Well, you just made a pretty good start on that yourself. Don't stand up. You haven't answered me. Denial or contrition?

A long pause.

Clifford   There is an emotional concept you may be unfamiliar with. It's known as compassion.

Louise   I think it's fair to warn you if you plead for sympathy your liver will become part of that upholstery.

Clifford   I don't expect an ounce of compassion to correct the wretched vision of *your* blighted eyeballs. I was not referring to *your* compassion, but to my own.

Louise   I want your heart in my hand.

Clifford   You have no idea –

Louise   Your blood to my elbows!

Clifford   You have no notion, and not the least ability to conceive, of the *pain* she suffered.

Louise   She needed *help*.

Clifford   She was as far beyond help as you are undeserving of it.

Louise   And love . . . ?

Clifford   . . . meant nothing to her. She was weighed down in a mire of self-hatred like a kitten in a sack. Alone in the dark with the bricks of her depression, which certainly knew no compassion. She could not recognise affection, she could not find the slightest comfort in the gentlest word, the tenderest touch. Because she could no longer *feel*. If it was not a dull unendurable pain, she could not feel it. I could have embraced her for a thousand days and for not one moment would she not have been alone. If I'd had true compassion, yes. I would have done it for her.

Abigail *plays, loud, atonal.* **Louise** *cocks the gun.* **Abigail** *stops playing.*

Clifford   As more than once she begged me to.

Pause. The gun shakes, settles down . . .

You think you know madness? You think your unstable little performances are some kind of credential? Your self-pity some kind of comparable disease? You have no idea. Your suffering's a construct; the problem and the solution, symbiotic. A vantage point from which to damage others. A hiding place from which you leap like an assassin. You think suffering's a bubonic sore you can cure by infecting other people. Well, that's not suffering; that's anger and spite and good old selfishness. You do all three spectacularly well, but it's not the real thing. The real thing isn't a neon crown of thorns. It's not a weapon you can use to terrorise everyone around you. It's a nail through your heart that never goes away and that no one can remove and you carry, silent, to the grave.

Louise   Did you or didn't you?

Clifford   Did I help Phoebe out of her misery?

Louise   Or out of yours?

Long pause.

Clifford   It was a bottle of Demerol. The gun was her idea.

Louise *lowers the gun.*

Clifford   And if I'd had to spend every day since in a twelve-by-nine cell, and every day to come under fluorescent tubes in lieu of daylight, I'd do the same again.

He stands. **Louise** *doesn't move.* **Clifford** *goes upstairs.*

Clifford   I may sell this bloody house . . .

Louise   I'd hate to say I told you so.

She gets up and goes to the freshly varnished door. Tries to prise it open with her fingernails. **Abigail** *starts practising the same short phrase over and over again. Something insistent and damaged about the way she plays.*

Louise   Where's the screwdriver? Where are the bloody tools?

Abigail (*barely audible*)   I d . . .

Louise   Did it do the trick, Abi? A bit of Polyfilla and a tub of varnish?

Abigail (*barely audible*)   I w . . . I w . . .

Louise   *You* saw what I saw.

Abigail (*barely audible*)   No, I d . . .

Louise   We saw what we *saw*.

Abigail   I don't remember!

She pushes through the phrase and beyond.

Louise   That's it. Play louder. Play until you can't hear yourself *think*.

Abigail *stops playing.*

Abigail   *I* wanted to go to her. That night. I said I *w* . . . *ant* to go to Mummy. You said I wasn't to. *You* said I mustn't.

Louise   Don't you think –

Abigail   I would have *gone* to her; you m . . . ade me not.

Louise   Don't you think you've punished me enough?

Abigail   When have I p . . . ?

Louise   I'm like a sodden sponge – I can't absorb any more of your *guilt*.

Abigail   I don't –

Louise   Of course you don't!

Abigail   I don't feel that.

Louise   Because you let me feel it *for* you!

Abigail   Nothing to feel g—

Louise   All these years. Like I'd been surgically removed from you with only guilt to cauterise the wound. Never enough of it, poured inside like pitch.

Abigail   Please d . . . d . . . d . . .

Louise   'Duh duh duh don't!' It's only possible to persecute the innocent, Abigail. Which isn't what you are!

Abigail   I've n . . . (ever)

Louise   I can't be this any more!

Abigail   I n . . . (eed you) I n . . . (eed you)

Louise   It's fucking killing me. You live here, looked after, fawned on. I live in terrible rooms and damp vans. Intolerable places. Freedom? It's a fucking miserable life. You play. I can't play; I try something else, whatever I try I can't . . . I'm *mediocre*. I should leave you here to rot. Pile up the newspapers, hoard the cats, turn into a mad fucking spinster, because if you're waiting for Ray –

Abigail   I'm no—

Louise   Cos, Jesus Christ, Abi, if he was ever going to reciprocate he'd have fucking done it by now.

Abigail   I d—

Louise   *In loco parentis*, he thinks, but he's just not got the balls. You'll wait for ever.

Abigail   I'm not w—

Louise   If you want him, drop your fucking knickers!

Abigail   It's n . . . It's n . . .

Louise   But in your head it is.

Abigail   He's not . . . He w . . .

Louise   Wouldn't what?

Abigail   Even if that's w . . . He w . . . He's not that sort of p . . .

Louise   Well, I beg to differ.

Abigail   He l . . . He l . . .

Louise   I'm sure he does. I'm sure he adores you, Abi. I'm sure he listens in rapture to every note you play. But it's me he fucks.

Silence.

Which I'm sure you knew.

Louise *goes out. The sound of a thousand chattering starlings can be heard outside. Or are they inside* **Abigail***'s head? She gets up. Crosses the room. Crosses back. Plays two notes. Changes her mind, crosses back.*

Makes up her mind, goes to the piano, sits, puts the tips of the fingers of her left hand on the keys, and with her right, slams down the piano lid. Her face contorts in a silent howl. She cradles her fingers. When the pain has subsided . . . she does it again.

Blackout.

Scene Two

Very early the next morning. It's cold and wet outside, the rain hammering down. The front door stands wide open. **Dawn** *comes down the stairs with luggage, wondering why the room's so cold. She sees the front door, crosses to close it and sees someone in the driveway beyond.*

Dawn   Excuse me? None of my business, but why are you standing out there? It's *raining*.

She finds a cigarette.

Blithering madhouse.

She goes back to the door.

Why don't you come inside? You'll get hypothermia; that'll be another trip to casualty.

Ray *comes inside. He's not wearing much.*

Dawn   You're soaked to the skin. Get out of those clothes. Go on – I've seen it all before.

Ray *strips down.* **Dawn** *looks out of the door.*

Dawn   Ever stood in a tropical storm, Ray?

Ray *shakes his head.*

Dawn   S'magnificent.

Ray   More a steady drizzle sort of man.

She closes the door.

Dawn   Our flight's at midday. I don't know if I should cancel. Give us those. I'll put them in the tumble dryer. Thought you were the sane one.

She leaves him in his underpants. He thinks about getting a drink.

A car pulls up outside. **Louise** *appears.*

Louise   They're back.

Ray   Stay in your room.

Louise *heads back upstairs and crumples on the landing.* **Ray** *goes out of the front door.* **Dawn** *comes back from the kitchen.*

Clifford (*off*)   Good grief, man – get inside.

Ray (*off*)   No problem.

Clifford (*off*)   Get under this.

Ray (*off*)   I'm fine.

Clifford (*off*)   Out she gets, then . . . out you get . . . easy does it . . . steady. Bloody paparazzi still at the gate . . . weather serves 'em right.

Ray *and* **Clifford** *enter, supporting* **Abigail** *and the umbrella above her. Her left hand is bruised, bandaged and splinted. In her right hand, an ice pack.*

Clifford   That's my girl. Easy does it.

They sit **Abigail** *on the sofa.*

Clifford   She's fine.

Ray   How are you?

Clifford   She's OK. Little bit sedated.

Ray   Yeah?

Clifford   Why are you . . . ?

Ray   What?

Dawn   He's sick of farming. I was giving him a few modelling tips.

Clifford   Are you packed?

Dawn   Flight's at twelve.

Clifford   Might be tight.

Dawn   We'll see. I'll put the kettle on.

She goes into the kitchen.

Clifford   You know, people berate the NHS, but I was sitting there in the wee small hours and I was very impressed. We should get you straight to bed, young lady. I slept a little in one of those vile plastic chairs, but mostly I was thinking. I'd like you both to know I blame myself for this. It was stupid of me, to plan a celebration here. I thought it would bring some life to the place. I thought you'd enjoy it, Abigail. In any case, it's given me food for thought. I think on the whole I made an appalling mistake when I kept this house. It isn't good for you. So I think what we'll do is find you somewhere else to live. We'll find you somewhere Louise can't find you, and we'll find you better care.

Abigail (*quietly*)   Ray?

Ray   She wouldn't want that.

Clifford   Obviously she's not in the best frame of mind, right now, to have any firm opinions. Equally obviously our current arrangements are less than satisfactory.

Ray   She copes, Clifford; she functions.

Clifford   Well, that's my point entirely, Ray. Quite evidently, she doesn't.

Ray   But if you chuck us out, who's going to work the farm?

Clifford   I'm selling the farm.

Ray   Y'what?

Clifford   I'm selling.

Abigail   Ray, w—

Ray   You can't do that.

Abigail   But wh—

Clifford   Of course I can.

Abigail   Where w—

Ray   What happens to us?

Clifford   Well, you can fly home. We've taken too great an advantage of your good nature, but the fact remains that you're not qualified to deal with this. Abi needs better care, don't you, sweetheart? It's time you said goodbye to Ray, and this house. A new start, Abi. What do you think?

Ray   She can't have an opinion when she's half unconscious.

Clifford   Look at her, Ray.

Ray   Wait till she's awake. Wait till she's smiling, slopping about in gumboots with a rabbit under her arm . . . then tell her she belongs in an institution.

Clifford   Don't exaggerate.

Ray   That's what they call those places, Clifford.

Clifford   Look at her hands, Ray. Look at her hands.

Ray   Well, it's your stupid bloody fault. We were rubbing along fine, we were coping.

Clifford   And every time Louise makes an appearance, Abigail relapses.

Ray   There's nothing wrong with Abigail!

Clifford   She has two fractured fingers, a dislocated thumb and extensive bruising. I'm not about to buy into the myth that she fell and tried to catch herself. She self-harmed.

Abigail   I d—

Clifford   She needs taking care of.

Ray   Well, instead of expecting strangers to do it, why don't you look after her yourself?

Clifford (*calmly*)   I tried that once before. With Phoebe. The outcome, as we know, couldn't have been worse.

Abigail (*barely audible*)   Please don't p . . . I w . . . I w . . .

Clifford   Don't upset yourself.

Abigail   P . . . lease?

Clifford   You need sleep.

Abigail   Mmmmmmmm?

Clifford   Close your eyes. Get some rest.

Abigail   Mmmm.

Clifford   I'm going to make things better.

She closes her eyes but opens them again as **Clifford** *crosses to* **Ray**.

Clifford   If Louise weren't part of the equation –

Ray   I can't control Louise.

Clifford   You indulge Louise. You encourage her. You both do. If you chose to do the opposite, perhaps yes, life here could continue with some semblance of sanity.

Ray   Jesus, Clifford.

Clifford   It stops here, Ray. This hereditary delicacy bollocks, this tainted thinking. Abigail needs to get well, and if Louise insists on being part of the disease, I'm washing my hands of her.

Ray   You don't like Louise much, do you, Clifford?

Clifford   I don't think I'm supposed to, Ray. I think that's her *raison d'être*.

Dawn *comes in with a mug of tea.*

Dawn   Should I cancel the flight?

Clifford   Well, you could go. I could follow tomorrow.

Dawn   I don't mind.

Ray   Both go. You might as well both go. I'll look after her.

Dawn   If we *are* going, it kind of has to be now.

Clifford   Well . . .

Ray   Go, Clifford. It's peace and quiet she needs.

Clifford   What do you think, sweetheart?

Abigail   Mmm?

Clifford   I'm happy to stay.

Abigail   No. Go.

Dawn   You're packed.

Clifford   Yes. Right.

Dawn   If you're sure.

Clifford   Are we sure?

Ray   I'm sure.

Clifford   Yes, then.

Dawn   I'll get the rest of the stuff.

Clifford   Thank you.

Dawn *goes upstairs.*

Clifford   I'd rather not leave the limo at Stansted. Can I take the four-by-four?

Ray   If you like. I'll take the pigs to market in the back of the Mercedes.

Clifford   Mm?

Ray   I'll get it out the barn.

Ray *goes outside.*

Clifford   You were unconscious, I think, but the consultant said it's not out of the question for you to play again. But if this were to happen a third time it's unlikely you'd be so lucky. I know you think she's the strong one, but she's not. I'll be back in a month. We'll see how the land lies. But if I get back and she's still here, this damaging little idyll is coming to an end.

Dawn, *carrying cases, come downstairs.*

Dawn   It's funny really; I had images of coming in here and hitting it off with everyone and somehow just, you know . . . resolving things. Stupid.

Clifford   We'll drive out the back way. There's a lane along the bottom field, and a five-bar.

Dawn   Righto. (*To* **Abigail**.) Goodbye, Louise.

Clifford   Abigail.

Dawn   Sh . . . Sorry. Abigail. I wanted to say to you something I once thought. I was off down memory lane one afternoon and it dawned on me about memories; all memories are of innocence.

Clifford   What are you trying to say?

Dawn   I've said it.

Abigail   Daddy?

Clifford   Sweetheart?

Dawn   Don't be long. God, those fucking birds.

She leaves with luggage.

Clifford   What is it?

Abigail   What if I was g . . . ood?

Clifford   You are good.

Abigail   I am good. Ray can stay?

Clifford   We'll see.

Abigail   He can, b . . . b . . . (ecause) (*Quietly.*) It wasn't me. It was Louise.

Clifford   It was Louise what?

Abigail   Hurt my hand.

Clifford   Is that so?

Abigail *nods her head.*

Clifford　Well, then. What I would suggest is, no more Louise.

He kisses her forehead.

Be good.

He leaves, taking luggage. **Abigail** *sits motionless.*

One repeated piano note plays from a distance, rising, coming closer, growing alarming. **Louise** *comes down the stairs.*

Louise (*fast, fractured*)　I'm going to go to the papers, one of them, don't know which, doesn't matter, he loves the spotlight, public eye, well, people should know, shouldn't people know? There isn't a secret ever kept that should have been kept. The nature of secrets is they shouldn't be secrets. They're poison. It'll hurt, yes, but him, it'll hurt him, who it's supposed to hurt, not you, not me. And yes, he'll, it'll, I want to say ruin, it'll ruin him, is that too harsh, and all this, but all this'll have to go, all this'll tumble down, but that's all right. It's only a roof and there's plenty of them . . . you'll be all right, because you and Ray . . . listen. You and Ray. It was only once. You and Ray should run away. One stupid time. Twice then, but it's you and Ray should . . . I want you both to . . . I know, his wife and, but he's not there, he's never going back. He loves you. It's the you in me he, me he never really . . . it's you he . . . we could all of us, the three of us, the two of you together, and me, as usual, I don't know. I'll busk. We'll . . . Abigail?

Abigail *looks up.*

Louise　Come with me.

Abigail (*hoarse, almost a whisper*)　Where?

Louise　I don't know.

Abigail　So why w . . . ould I?

Louise　There's always somewhere. I get lonely.

Abigail　You'd abandon me.

Louise　I wouldn't.

Abigail   It's just dreams.

Louise   How can it be dreams? I've lived them.

Abigail   Your life's a nightmare. That's why you come back.

Louise   I come back for you.

Ray *comes in from outside with the shotgun.*

Ray   Poor old Blanche. In the middle of the drive as usual.

Louise   Put her out of her misery.

Ray   There's a fair amount of it if you look her in the eye. Anyway, Clifford's gone. It'll all blow over. Oh, and I've been on the phone to Edwin. The hawk died. Chicken flu. I love the country. I love that dog.

Ray *goes into the kitchen, laying the shotgun on the piano.*

Louise   Come on, Abi. Let's run away.

Abigail   I want to stay here.

Louise   I know.

Abigail   So you have to go.

Pause.

Louise *goes to the piano and plays one lonely half of 'Chopsticks'.*

Abigail *doesn't move.*

Louise   Let's make a book like the one we once made. With our whole lives in it. You were going to ride a whale and play the Albert Hall, and get married to an Arab prince, and I was going to set fire to a few things and read the news and, I'm proud to say, *invent* Rollerblades, I think. Let's start another one.

Abigail   You mustn't come back.

Long pause.

You have to n . . . ot come back.

Ray *comes in from the kitchen.*

Ray   What the fuck is this?

Louise   Clifford's passport.

Ray   What the fuck were you thinking?

Louise   I wasn't really.

Ray   The four-by-four's on its way back, you stupid bitch. We were rid of him.

Louise   Just a bit of petty spite, Ray. No need to throw a paddy.

Ray   If there's a moment's peace, a moment's possibility, you fuck it up. Your father's right, we'd be better off without you.

Louise   Is that what you think?

Ray   Well, for Christ's sake, look at her! You don't just cause trouble, you do damage. You do actual physical damage.

Louise   You're right. I shouldn't have done that. Sometimes I do things. Things I wish I hadn't. I'm so sorry, Abigail. I'll go then, shall I?

Ray   Why don't you?

He puts his arm around **Abigail***.*

Louise   All very touching, Ray, but *in loco parentis* isn't quite your style, is it? Unless that includes having your cock sucked.

Abigail *moans and starts to run upstairs.*

Ray   Abi. Abi!

He grabs her, accidentally hurting her hand. She howls.

Jesus, sorry, sweetheart.

She collapses.

I'm sorry.

Louise   I think you hurt her, Ray.

Ray   It was stupid. It was years ago.

Louise   We're none of us immune.

Ray   Oh, fuck off, Louise. Take your bile and your anger and your spite and just fuck off. Abigail goes under every time you're here. Now for Christ's sake leave her alone before you kill her.

He embraces **Abigail***, rocking her tenderly.* **Louise** *plays one note, repeatedly. The sound of a vehicle pulling up in the drive. Suddenly, unseen by* **Ray** *and* **Abigail***,* **Louise** *takes the gun and goes out.*

Ray   We're gonna be OK. I'm here for you. I swear to God. I'm here for good. Get you better. Get you well again. Couple of wheelchairs and a stairlift, we'll be fine and dandy here for years.

Abigail *laughs. They look to one another and then, for the first time, they kiss. A gunshot. The starlings stunned to silence.*

Ray   She's frightening the birds.

Abigail   But listen. They haven't gone.

Ray *walks to the window.*

Lights change to isolate **Ray***. We hear his disembodied voice . . .*

Ray   . . . that the gun was fired to disperse the starlings? Which had roosted overlong . . . was fired at the dog, to put the devoted old bitch out of her misery . . . the gun was fired in anger . . . was fired accidentally . . . deliberately . . . into a mind that yearned for it . . . an attempt to articulate everything . . . in the momentary embrace . . . of nothing.

He speaks.

A shot that kills has a certain echo to it, and this had none. But before the silen—

A second, louder shot. **Ray** *looks over at* **Abigail** *as we hear the thousand starlings lift as one, the feathering of their wings swiftly rising to a flurry and a crescendo of sound. The shadows of the flock flicker in the steely sunlight that slants through the French windows. It grows in density until, as* **Ray** *looks back and with an almighty crash, the window gives* *way. The room fills with starlings. The birds tornado around* **Abigail** *and* **Ray**. *She escapes the piano. The birds become so dense, the room is obliterated. Their cacophony reaches a crescendo and in the darkness, suddenly, stops.*

Light isolates **Abigail** *at the piano. Her arm cast has disappeared. She plays Ravel's 'Pavanne for a Dead Child'. She plays beautifully.*